TRUE CRIME CASE HISTORIES

VOLUME 6

JASON NEAL

AKAMAI PUBLISHING

Cover photos of:

David Parker (top-left)

Donald Smith (top-right)

Kenneth Biros (bottom-left)

Sandy Murphy (bottom-right)

More books by Jason Neal

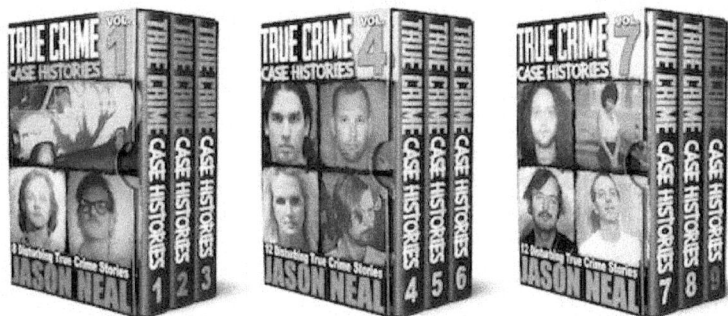

Looking for more?? I am constantly adding new volumes of True Crime Case Histories. The series **can be read in any order,** and all books are also available in paperback, hardcover, and audiobook.

Check out the complete series on Amazon

https://amazon.com/author/jason-neal

or

JasonNealBooks.com

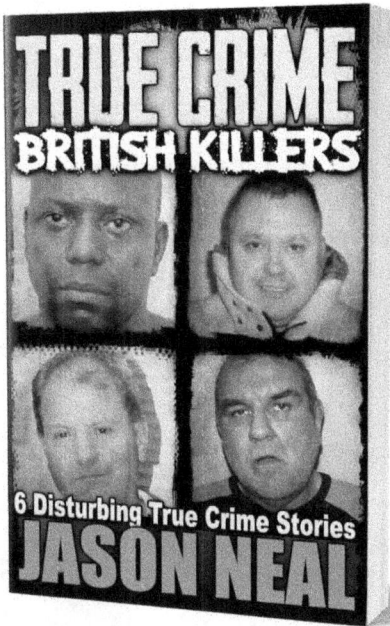

FREE Bonus Book
For My Readers

Click to get
your free copy!

As my way of saying "Thank you" for downloading, I'm giving away a FREE true crime book I think you'll enjoy.

https://TrueCrimeCaseHistories.com

Just click the link above to let me know where to send your free book!

Choose Your Free True Crime Audiobook

Add Audible Narration and Keep the Story Going!
Plus Get a FREE True Crime Audiobook!

Switch between listening to an audiobook and reading on your Kindle.
Plus choose your first audiobook for FREE!

https://geni.us/AudibleTrueCrime

CONTENTS

INTRODUCTION

As with the previous volumes of True Crime Case Histories, I use this introduction space as a quick word of warning. The stories in this book represent humanity at its absolute worst. Pure evil. Television crime shows and news articles often skip the messy parts of true crime stories. The details are just too much for the average viewer or reader.

In my books, however, I don't leave out the details. I go through hours of research for each story. I search through old newspaper articles, court documents, first-hand descriptions, and autopsy reports. In my books I include details not to shock, but to give the reader a deeper look into the twisted mind of the killer. In the end, it's unlikely any of us will understand the motive of the criminals in these books, but the level of depravity will at least keep you turning pages.

That being said, if you are overly squeamish with the details of true crime, this book may not be for you. If you're okay with it... then let's proceed.

———

Volume Six of True Crime Case Histories features twelve new stories from the past several decades. There's the story of a young English man that had plans to become the UK's most notorious serial killer, but couldn't keep his mouth shut after his first kill and bragged to over twenty of his friends.

Another story covers a group of four young men who believed they could do anything they wanted because their lord Satan protected them. Satan apparently couldn't protect them from prison.

There's the story of a San Diego man who made it his life's mission to help young men avoid a life of crime. His good deeds resulted in his entire family being butchered by a boy he was trying to help.

Another killer, a father of eight children, lured women to his boat, raped them, and threw them overboard. Ingenious forensic science was eventually used to catch the killer.

One story of a young man that couldn't handle being rejected by his teenage girlfriend was suggested to me by a reader whose daughter had a close-call with the killer.

The twelve stories in this volume are shocking and disturbing, but they're true. These things really happen in the world. We may never understand why killers do what they do, but at least we can be better informed.

You may have heard of a few of the stories in this volume, but there are several I'm almost certain you haven't. My goal is to find stories that aren't already covered all over the Internet. Over the last few volumes, many of my readers have sent me cases they remembered happening in their hometowns. If you have any stories that are largely unreported, please send them my way. I thrive on digging through old newspapers and trying to research interesting stories.

Lastly, please join my mailing list for discounts, updates, and a free book. You can sign up for that at

TrueCrimeCaseHistories.com

You can also purchase paperbacks, hardcovers, and signed copies of my books directly from me at:

JasonNealBooks.com

Additional photos, videos, and documents pertaining to the cases in this volume can be found on the accompanying web page listed at the end of this book.

Thank you for reading. I sincerely hope you gain some insight from this volume of True Crime Case Histories.

- Jason

CHAPTER 1
LOST IN THE DESERT

Anyone that lived in the Phoenix, Arizona area in the nineties might remember Terri's Consignment & Design. The commercials were shown constantly on television throughout the Phoenix valley and featured Terri Bowersock and her mother, Loretta Bowersock.

Loretta had run a successful furniture store as a young woman. In 1983, she used her business acumen to help her daughter, Terri, start her own furniture consignment company with a $2,000 loan from Terri's grandmother. Terri's Consignment & Design stores featured "gently used" furniture at bargain prices. Within a few years, the stores were well known throughout the Phoenix area and Terri was making a fortune.

Despite growing up with dyslexia, Terri was a master at marketing her business and was awarded the title of Arizona's top businesswoman. Not long afterward, Avon awarded her their prestigious "Woman of Enterprise" award and she was featured on the Oprah Winfrey show in an episode featuring "unexpected millionaires."

Loretta and Terri Bowersock in one of their commercials.

Although Terri owned the business, Loretta also became wealthy and bought a large house in the Phoenix suburb of Tempe. As a single woman, however, the home was too large for her and she decided to rent out a room in 1986. Loretta placed a classified ad in the local paper reading, "Room for lease in nice home. Executive businesswoman." The first person to respond was a forty-nine-year-old man named Taw Benderly.

Benderly showed up to her home penniless and with nothing but the shirt on his back. He told fifty-one-year-old Loretta that he had literally just gotten off of a plane at the airport and had his bag stolen. Loretta felt sorry for him and let him stay.

Benderly was tall, charming, and intelligent. He spoke in a way that was impressive, persuasive, and very convincing. He told her he had grown up as an only child, but his parents had died when he was young, leaving his grandmother to raise him. After high-school he went to college and received a master's degree in business.

It didn't take long before Loretta had fallen in love with her new roommate. In the following years, Loretta continued to work with her daughter while Benderly tinkered in the garage. He had convinced himself that he could become an inventor and was full of ideas that he claimed would be "the next big thing." He worked on projects such as a "revolutionary" lawn mower blade, a solar-energy unit, and a shield to keep cars cool in the Arizona heat. Unfortunately, none of his ideas ever seemed to work out.

Loretta combed through garage sales and estate sales. She looked for watches and jewelry that she could refurbish and resell at a profit. Meanwhile, Benderly toyed with his inventions, cooked, and cleaned the house. Although he didn't bring home any income, from the outside it seemed that the couple were fine that way. In reality, however, it was far from okay.

By the early nineties, Benderly convinced Loretta that she was entitled to a much larger stake in Terri's furniture business and encouraged her to sue her daughter. The lawsuit took years and drove a wedge between the mother and daughter team. The dispute was eventually resolved, but it had been a very difficult time for Loretta emotionally.

As the years pressed on, Benderly became condescending towards Loretta. He constantly put her down and made her feel inadequate. The abuse crumbled her self-esteem. Her bookshelves were filled with self-help books and video recordings of Oprah and Dr. Phil episodes about how to save a relationship and domestic abuse.

Loretta had confided in her daughter and sisters that her life with Taw Benderly wasn't ideal. However, as a woman in her sixties, she believed it was too late to leave him and start anew. She and Benderly had promised each other early in their relationship that they would grow old together; she was intent on keeping that promise.

Benderly talked incessantly at family get-togethers about the income potential of his pet projects. Terri was receptive and for years gave him $20,000 to $40,000 per year to help get his inventions off the ground. She had no idea that other friends, neighbors, and relatives were loaning him money too.

―――

At 6:00 p.m. on December 14, 2004, Taw Benderly walked up to the security desk at the Park Place Mall in Tucson, Arizona, in a frenzy. He told mall security that he had dropped Loretta off at the Dillard's Department Store at 2:00 p.m. that day. He had planned on picking her up at 4:00 p.m., but had spent the last two hours walking through the mall looking for her. She was nowhere to be found.

That evening, police searched through the Dillard's store, the mall, and the surrounding neighborhood, but found no sign of Loretta. The police were familiar with Loretta's name because they had seen her and Terri on their television commercials. Initially, they thought she had possibly been abducted and was being held for ransom.

Benderly explained to detectives that he and Loretta Bower-sock, his partner of eighteen years, had planned on coming to Tucson for a five-day vacation and to do some Christmas shopping. He claimed that he and Loretta left Tempe at 10:00 a.m. and drove to Tucson. They checked into the Tucson Residence Inn at 12:30 p.m. before he dropped her off at the mall at 2:00 p.m.

It didn't take long for police to find holes in his story. The mall security tapes were the first inconsistency. After poring through the security tapes of both Dillard's and the rest of the store, there was no trace of Benderly looking for Loretta for two hours as he said. Instead, he had parked his maroon mini-van in the parking lot at 6:00 p.m. and walked straight to the security desk. There was also no footage of Loretta in the mall at all that day.

With a warrant, police searched Benderly's hotel room. Inside they found various valuables: expensive watches, necklaces, and rings. He had also brought several guns and ammunition. He packed eight suitcases for the five-day trip, but only one suitcase contained any of Loretta's clothes. The rest were his own belongings.

However, what troubled police the most was what they found when they searched his maroon mini-van. In the back of the van was a pickaxe and shovel, both caked with dirt. They also found a box of miscellaneous pieces of rope and a map of the desert area between Phoenix and Tucson. This discovery was more than just a red flag.

Tucson detectives contacted Tempe police for a warrant to search Benderly and Loretta's home. Inside their garage was another mini-van. In the back of the van police found a purse containing Loretta's identification, checkbook, and credit cards. In a trash can outside of the house was a paper towel with a small amount of blood on it. It was clear to Tucson police that Loretta never made it to Tucson alive.

Taw Benderly & Loretta Bowersock

With good reason, police didn't believe Benderly's story and brought him in for questioning. During the interview he was combative and showed more concern for the accusations against him than finding Loretta:

> "You need to respect that the fact that I'm trying to give you information in as clear a form as I can. I was not prepared to have to account minute for minute for my time."

Tucson detectives were convinced that Benderly had killed Loretta and most likely buried her in the desert somewhere between Tempe and Tucson. Benderly eventually refused to speak further with police and, without a body, they were unable to charge him for anything. They were forced to release him.

Investigators began backtracking Benderly's movements of the day Loretta went missing. He claimed they left Tempe at 10:00 a.m. that day and checked into the hotel at 12:30. At 2:00 p.m., he dropped her off at the mall. Hotel records at the Residence

Inn, however, showed the check-in at 2:48 p.m. – and the hotel staff said Benderly checked-in alone. There was no record of Loretta in the hotel.

Benderly's credit card and cell phone records also told a different story of the day. He had used a credit card to purchase two baseball caps at 11:00 a.m. at an outlet mall in Casa Grande, just south of Phoenix. At 12:30 p.m. he returned a cell phone call to his dentist. The call used a cell phone tower near exit 199, also near Casa Grande. Finally, at 1:15 p.m., he purchased two sandwiches at the Love's truck stop just a mile further down the interstate.

The time between 11:00 a.m. and 1:15 p.m. remained unaccounted for. Police believed that after he left the outlet mall, he buried Loretta in the desert somewhere nearby before continuing down to Tucson.

———

Terri Bowersock was distraught at the disappearance of her mother and confronted Benderly personally. Despite the inconsistencies, he insisted he had nothing to do with Loretta's disappearance.

Terri didn't know what to think. Having had close contact with the Phoenix area television stations and newspapers, she turned to them for help. The story of Loretta's disappearance became front-page news. The media attention incited friends and strangers to help her search the area between Phoenix and Tucson. Although Benderly's call had bounced off of a particular cell phone tower, the area covered by that tower was an enormous area of desert; finding a body in that large of an area was highly unlikely.

The story also attracted psychics who claimed they could help. Terri was a believer in the supernatural and hired eight different psychics for advice. The psychics provided her with tips that were mostly available to anyone that read the newspapers. One particular psychic, however, convinced Terri that she could talk to the dead. The clairvoyant told her she needed to check on the whereabouts of Taw Benderly.

Tucson police were building their case against Benderly and were close to having enough evidence to arrest him. They had gone through his and Loretta's financial records and found that he had taken out several large loans using her name. He had also embezzled money from her company and hadn't been making the mortgage payments. Together, they were tens of thousands of dollars in debt and Loretta's beautiful Tempe home was just days away from foreclosure. Phone records showed she had made seventeen calls to the bank the day before she disappeared.

Terri hadn't spoken to Benderly in the past few days and went to check on him. After there was no answer at his door and he wasn't answering phone calls, she called the police.

On December 22, just eight days after Loretta went missing, Tempe police entered Benderly's home to find him dead. He had hanged himself using an extension cord tied to rafters in the garage. Benderly had left a suicide note, but it said nothing of Loretta's whereabouts or how she died. It only said,

> "Loretta and I vowed over the years that we would spend eternity together, and so we shall."

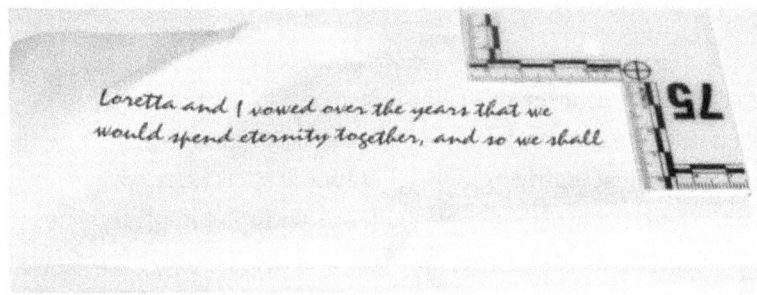

Loretta and I vowed over the years that we would spend eternity together, and so we shall

Taw Benderly suicide note

Though Loretta and Terri had been told by Benderly that his parents were dead and he was raised by his grandmother, Terri soon found out this story was a lie. Benderly not only had a brother, but his mother and father were still alive. He also had an ex-wife and two children that he hadn't spoken to in over eighteen years. His story of having a master's degree in business was a lie too. In fact, when he showed up at Loretta's doorstep eighteen years earlier, he had only recently been released from prison for theft.

———

It appeared that any hopes of finding Loretta's body had vanished with the death of Taw Benderly. The only remaining clues came from psychics with vague descriptions like; "look for something red in the dirt," "she's in the desert," or "she's buried next to something blue." But Terri still put her faith in the psychics, even inviting one to help her hike through the desert looking for her mother.

Six months after she went missing, police called off the official search for Loretta Bowersock. Nonetheless, Terri continued to spend her weekends hiking through the desert south of Phoenix.

———

Just over a year after she went missing, two hikers kicked at a rock in the desert and uncovered part of a human skull. When police dug just eighteen inches below the surface, they unearthed a complete female skeleton wrapped in plastic bags. One bag covered her head, another was shoved down her throat.

Loretta Bowersock's remains found in the desert

Dental records proved that the body was that of Loretta Bowersock. A forensic examination determined that she most likely died of asphyxiation by placing a bag over her head. The body was buried without shoes, leading police to believe that she had died at their home in Tempe.

———

Terri Bowersock found solace in the discovery of her mother's body and that she could give her a proper burial. Rather than the police work involved, she credited the clairvoyant with finding her mother's remains. Today, the same psychic can be found on social media websites spouting dozens of unsubstantiated and easily debunked conspiracy theories.

The economic downturn wasn't kind to Terri Bowersock and her consignment stores. Three years after her mother's body was found, her multi-million dollar empire came crumbling down. The Better Business Bureau received 188 complaints in a matter of thirty-six months. Google and Yelp were filled with negative reviews of her businesses from people who put their furniture on consignment and never saw a dime in return.

The business she started with a $2,000 loan – which had grown to seventeen stores, employed 300 people, and made $36 million a year – eventually filed for bankruptcy protection. Terri Bowersock also filed for personal bankruptcy.

CHAPTER 2
CONSUMED BY DESIRE

Eighteen-year-old Heather Gibson was in her senior year at Loy Norrix High School in Kalamazoo when she first met Chadwick "Chad" Wiersma. The young and naive girl was thrilled that an older boy liked her, but it was his "bad boy" nature that intrigued her the most.

Chad was a stocky blonde that grew up in a middle-class family just outside of Kalamazoo, but he had a knack for getting into more trouble than his siblings. At twenty years old, although he had a job and an apartment of his own, he'd had a few brushes with the law which eventually resulted in a felony conviction.

When Heather and Chad first began dating in 1993, she lived with her parents and younger sister in a quiet neighborhood on the south side of Kalamazoo, Michigan. Though Heather was smitten with him, her parents could tell that the young man was trouble. Her father, Robert Gibson, knew Chad wasn't an ordinary kid. Robert tried to convince his daughter that she should avoid Chad and concentrate on school, but it was too late. Like any teenage girl, she was deep into her schoolgirl crush.

However, her father was right. It only took a few months before Heather realized that the relationship with Chad wasn't going to work. When she told him she thought they should start seeing other people, Chad became enraged. He forced her into her car and told her to drive. They drove to a remote location where he berated her.

Chad exploded in anger, telling her she absolutely couldn't leave him. He threatened her and told her he would kill her and her family if she ever left him. Heather pleaded with him for hours before he eventually calmed down, but it was only temporary.

Heather reluctantly agreed to continue dating Chad, but his obsessive jealousy continued. He constantly watched every move she made. He repeatedly accused her of flirting with other young men. The couple constantly argued and it all came to a boiling point in December 1993. She told him it was over, turned her back on him, and walked to her car.

In a rage, Chad pulled his own car in behind hers in the parking lot so she couldn't drive away. He got out of the car and stomped over to her driver side window and screamed at her through the glass. Although Heather tried to calm him down, it was no use. His mind was gone in a testosterone-fueled rage. Using a large rock, Chad smashed her driver's side window and dragged her out of the car, onto the pavement.

After a crowd of witnesses gathered around, she managed to calm him down. She screamed at him that it was over for good this time. He eventually moved his car and Heather drove away. At home, Heather's father was livid and stressed his point that Chad was trouble. She really needed to end their relationship for good.

Chad Wiersma & Heather Gibson (high school photos) / Chad Wiersma (mugshot)

For the next four months, Heather managed to stay away from Chad – but he was persistent and persuasive. By the spring of 1994 they'd made up and she had moved in with him. She was convinced he had really changed this time. Heather's father, however, wasn't as forgiving. He made it clear that Chad was never to be welcome in their home.

Over the next two years, Heather and Chad's relationship was a yo-yo. They broke up, got back together, and broke up again so many times that their friends lost count. But finally, in February 1996, Heather broke it off with him one last time. She moved out of his apartment and back home with her parents. This time it was for good.

Chad was not one to accept rejection. Over the next month, he obsessively asked friends if she was dating someone else. He asked them to spy on her and couldn't stand the thought that she could be with another man. Each time he called her at home, her father would answer and immediately hang up on him.

Chad grew frustrated that he couldn't talk to Heather and had heard rumors that she was dating someone new. His drug and alcohol use fueled his rage until, eventually, he couldn't take any more.

In late March he asked his co-worker, Robert Burr, multiple times to call the house, ask for Heather, and then hand the phone to him. When that trick no longer worked, Chad asked him to help him get a gun.

Robert knew that with Chad's prior felony, he couldn't legally possess a gun. He knew helping Chad get a gun was a crime and turned him down. Chad was desperate. He asked other co-workers, but all knew of his prior record and refused to help him.

On April 1, Chad visited with a friend, Eric Edgerson. Eric had been cleaning a 9 millimeter pistol that evening as the two of them drank gin and orange juice, smoked pot, and snorted some cocaine. When he finished cleaning the gun, he set it on top of a stereo speaker.

Later in the evening, Chad grabbed the gun off of the speaker and fired it inside the house. Eric screamed at him, "What the fuck are you doing?!" Chad only laughed and claimed it went off by accident. He set the gun back down and the two continued partying.

By the early morning hours, Chad was too drunk and high to go home so he slept on the couch. When Eric woke up the next morning, Chad and the gun were gone.

———

Eric drove to Kalamazoo to look for Chad and the gun. He too knew that Chad wasn't allowed to carry a gun. Eric drove to both his apartment and his grandmother's house, but there was no sign of Chad or the gun. Knowing of his felony conviction and his rage toward Heather, Eric drove to the police station to report his gun stolen.

Late that morning, Chad drove to another co-worker's house. When he arrived at Brian Kirsch's house, Chad immediately started complaining about Heather. He was convinced she was flirting with other men. He ranted about Heather leaving him and how she wouldn't take his phone calls.

Brian, however, didn't take him seriously when Chad said he was "thinking about killing someone." Unfortunately, that would soon become a reality.

———

In the early afternoon, Chad Wiersma left Brian's house and drove to Heather's parents' house at 4039 Duke Street. Robert Gibson was working in the garage when Chad drove up. Before Heather's father had a chance to speak, Chad pulled the handgun from his pocket and motioned for Robert to go inside the house.

Once inside the house, Robert tried to calm him down but Chad screamed, "Shut your fucking mouth! Just keep walking into the kitchen." Robert walked into the kitchen, pulled out a chair from the kitchen table, and sat down. Robert desperately tried to settle him down, but there was no use. Chad's brain was boiling. He walked behind Robert, put the gun up to the back of his head, and fired. Robert Gibson fell to the floor, his body curled in the fetal position under the kitchen table, and bled out.

With Heather's father dead on the kitchen floor, Chad ransacked the rest of the house, starting with Heather's room. He was looking for evidence that Heather had been cheating on him. They had been broken up for two months, but in his mind he still considered it cheating. He ran from room to room emptying drawers onto the floor, but found nothing to satiate him.

Consumed with adrenaline, Chad sat behind the front door in the living room with the gun in his hand, waiting for Heather to get home from work.

A little after 3:00 p.m., the door opened – but it wasn't Heather. It was her younger sister, Rachel, with her friend Melanie. The two fourteen-year-old girls had recorded the latest episode of X-Files and were excited to watch it after school, but their plans came to a screeching halt. Chad pointed his gun at them as soon as they walked in the door and forced them to the floor. "Keep your eyes down! Don't look up!" he screamed. Chad didn't want them to see that Rachel and Heather's father lay in a pool of blood in the kitchen.

Chad screamed at Rachel, "I'm waiting for your mother to get home so I can kill your family all at once!" He then pushed the two young girls onto the living room couch and forced one to perform oral sex on him while training the gun on the other. For several hours Chad sodomized and tortured the two girls as Rachel cried for her father. All the while, he shielded the girls from seeing into the kitchen.

After almost two hours of abuse, Heather walked in the front door to a gun in her face. Chad immediately grabbed her and shoved her over by the two younger girls, then took all three girls into the front bedroom—away from the kitchen.

His jealousy took over and he screamed at Heather, questioning her about her social life and accusing her of flirting with other men. He and Heather argued for almost an hour when there was suddenly a knock on the door. Chad pointed the gun at the girls and told them to keep quiet. It was another friend of Rachel's that had arrived to watch X-Files with the other girls.

Eventually the knocking stopped and the young girl luckily escaped the ordeal. Chad told Heather that if she didn't go back with him, he would kill her entire family. Little did she know that her father was already dead.

Heather had a knack for calming Chad down and eventually bargained with him. She offered her own life for her family's. She told Chad she would go with him and he could kill her if he wanted to, but to spare the life of the rest of her family.

Chad placed the gun at her back and directed Heather toward her burgundy Pontiac Grand Prix. With Heather in the passenger seat, Chad drove down the street. Heather took her first opportunity to escape when he stopped at a stop light. She opened the door and ran as fast as she could, screaming at the top of her lungs. Chad panicked, stepped on the gas, and took off in her car.

When Heather ran back to her house, she and the other two girls discovered the body of Robert Gibson in the kitchen and called police.

Ninety minutes after Heather escaped, police received a call from Chad Wiersma. "I shot somebody and I don't know what to do," he told police dispatch. Chad told them he was at a convenience store and ready to give himself up. He reassured officers that the gun was in the trunk and the ammunition clip was in the glove box.

Police arrested Wiersma and put in the back of the squad car, where he immediately confessed that he had stolen the gun from a friend and had killed his ex-girlfriend's father.

At the murder scene, police collected the 9 millimeter metal-jacketed bullet and a shell casing. After test firing the gun retrieved from the trunk of the car, the ballistics test was a match. Police also obtained fingerprints from a drinking glass at the Gibson house that was a match to Chad Wiersma.

———

Wiersma was charged on twelve counts. One count of open murder, seven counts of first-degree criminal sexual conduct, assault with a dangerous weapon, two counts of committing a felony with a firearm, and being a felon in possession of a firearm.

After a psychiatric examination, it was determined that Wiersma was competent to stand trial. However, despite giving a full account of what happened during the questioning, he later claimed that he had no recollection of the events or anything that happened over the days prior to the murder.

———

The trial of Chad Wiersma began in October 1996. He pleaded guilty to seven of the charges, including all the sexual assault charges. This was good news for the prosecution, as the two fourteen-year-old girls could limit the amount of detail they would have to tell the court about the traumatic events.

Before Heather and Rachel Gibson testified about the ordeal, the judge ordered all spectators and media from the room. Only their mother was allowed to remain for support.

Heather explained how Wiersma was consumed by desire. She detailed his abuse dating back to the early days of their relationship, when he broke the car window and dragged her through it. She went on to explain the events of the day and his threats to murder her entire family.

Rachel told the court of the torture and abuse she endured as Wiersma threatened to kill her entire family while he raped her and her friend.

His defense attorney asked to have Wiersma's confession removed from the record, claiming that he hadn't been read his Miranda rights at the time. In court he changed his story and claimed that he hadn't told police that he shot anyone, but the Kalamazoo arresting officers testified that he voluntarily gave the statement about the killing.

The dispatch officer that took his phone call before his arrest also testified that he said, "I shot somebody and I don't know what to do."

Wiersma's friends also testified against him; his two co-workers and the friend from whom he stole the gun.

———

Regardless of his denials, Wiersma was going away for life no matter what. On November 19, 1995, Chadwick Robert Wiersma was found guilty of the remaining two charges, resulting in his guilt on all twelve charges.

Three of the rape charges received a sentence of 60 to 90 years. He received a life sentence each for the remaining four charges. The murder charge carried yet another life sentence. All of his sentences were harsher because of his habitual offender status.

CHAPTER 3
GAY PANIC

Gwen Amber Rose Araujo was born in 1985, but she wasn't born with that name. She was actually born Edward Araujo, Jr.

When he was just ten-months-old, Eddie Araujo's father disappeared after his parents divorced. Eddie spent his early childhood years like a normal kid in the Bay Area of California: he was into baseball, fishing, and camping. But his mother and sister both knew early on that Eddie was different. They didn't understand it… but they knew it.

Eddie never had a masculine side. Instead, he was extremely feminine in everything he did. At school he was ridiculed by many classmates, but despite it all, he was outgoing and had many friends that accepted him for who he was.

By the time Eddie was fourteen, he knew it was time. He couldn't pretend to be a boy any longer. Eddie let his mother know he was transgender and wanted to become a girl. From that point on, she asked to be referred to as Gwen after her favorite musician, Gwen Stefani. Although Gwen's mother accepted her new identity, she initially refused to call her by her new name.

Gwen proudly wore girl's clothes and makeup. Though the bullying at school increased, she still had plenty of friends who accepted her new look. It took immense courage to dress as she did in a suburban town. However, Gwen just felt so natural as a girl. She took such pride in playing the part that someone who had just met her would have a hard time realizing she was born male.

Gwen Araujo

Despite the support of her friends, the bullying got worse and worse. As a result, her grades suffered and eventually she dropped out of school. She was an expert at applying her makeup, so much so that many of her female friends regularly asked her to do their makeup for them. She had hopes of going to cosmetology school, moving to Hollywood, and becoming famous.

Finding a job proved difficult as well. Gwen looked convincingly like a girl. When the name on her job applications didn't match her appearance, she was usually turned down. By the time she turned seventeen, Gwen had planned to begin hormone treatment and undergo surgery to become a woman.

———

Gwen liked to party and, in the late summer of 2002, met several young men that enjoyed the same. José and Paul Merél were two brothers that rented a house in Newark, California, a small residential town midway between San Jose and Oakland near the south end of the bay.

José and Paul's house was known as a party house where teenagers and young adults would regularly drink alcohol and smoke marijuana. In late August, Gwen partied with José and his friends Michael Magidson, Jaron Nabors, and Jason Cazares.

All four men were in their late teens or early twenties and found seventeen-year-old Gwen to be an attractive young girl, albeit with a bit of a deep voice. She drank, smoked pot, and flirted with the young men throughout the night. When she left, Jaron turned to the other three, noted her deep voice, and jokingly said, "Could this be a dude?" All four laughed off the comment and didn't take it seriously.

During subsequent nights, Gwen returned to the house and continued partying and flirting with the young men. One evening she performed oral sex on Michael Magidson. On another night, during an encounter with José Merél, she told him she was having her period and pushed him away from her genitalia and toward her anus. They had anal sex without José realizing she was a man.

―――――

José's older brother, Paul, had been dating a girl named Nicole Brown who often partied at the house too. Nicole was a tomboy —a tough girl that liked to fight. She had never lost a fight to another girl... until she met Gwen.

Toward the end of a night of drinking, Nicole challenged Gwen to give the men in the room a striptease. The young men gathered around, but Gwen wanted no part in it. As Nicole egged her on, the challenge had escalated into hair pulling, shoves, and eventually a full-fledged fistfight.

In the end, the men pulled them apart. But Gwen had gotten the best of Nicole. Shocked that she received such powerful blows from a girl that was much smaller than her, Nicole told the men,

"She fought like a guy."

That night was the beginning of much speculation between the four men; José, Michael, Jaron, and Jason. Over the next two weeks, the men debated whether Gwen could actually be a boy. José and Michael, both of who had sexual encounters with her, were especially concerned. They questioned their own manhood. The four concluded that if she was indeed male...

"something bad could happen."

―――――

Two weeks later, on October 3, 2002, the four men were at a nightclub early in the evening. "I swear, if it's a fucking man, I'm gonna kill him. If it's a man, she ain't gonna leave," José told the other men. Michael replied, "I don't know what I'm gonna do."

Jaron added, "Whatever you do, make sure you don't make a mess."

Gwen was back at the house drinking and smoking with Nicole and José's brothers, Paul and Emmanuel, when the four young men returned home from the club after midnight. Michael and José were obsessed with the possibility that Gwen was male. They could think of nothing else.

A little after 3:30 a.m., Paul and Nicole were preparing to go to bed in the back bedroom when they heard a commotion in the kitchen. When Nicole came out she heard Michael confronting Gwen,

"Are you a man?! Are you a man?!"

Gwen stood in silence.

Nicole encouraged the confrontation and said, "Why don't one of you guys find out?" Michael's heart raced. He grabbed Gwen by the arm and pushed her into the bathroom. The others waited patiently in the kitchen while Michael and Gwen talked in the bathroom. But Nicole was an instigator - she couldn't wait any longer and went into the bathroom. Gwen was sleepy and drunk, sitting on the bathroom counter when Nicole grabbed Gwen's knees and spread her legs open. "It's a man! Oh my God!" she screamed.

When José heard those words, his stomach churned. He started crying and vomited near the bathroom while the other three men stormed out the door of the house to smoke cigarettes. "I can't be gay!" José repeated, over and over. Nicole tried to console him, but he was lost in a world of self-pity.

Nicole could see the blood boiling in the other three men and pleaded with them, "Let her go. Just let her walk out the door."

Feeling a bit of remorse that she encouraged all of this, Nicole went back to the bathroom and told Gwen, "You better run as fast as you can."

Gwen ran for the door, but Jaron blocked her path. Michael grabbed her, threw her to the ground, and sat on her chest, pinning her down. He screamed at her for a moment, then let her up.

Nicole knew something seriously bad was going to happen. Her boyfriend, Paul Merél, was on probation. She knew that if he was involved in anything that was about to happen, he would go back to jail. Nicole ran to the back room, grabbed Paul and his younger brother Emmanuel, and the three of them left before the situation spun further out of control.

Michael yanked down Gwen's skirt to show her genitals, then started punching her in the face. When she fell to the ground, he put her in a chokehold, but Jaron and Jason pulled him off.

When Gwen stood up, she said, "Please don't. I have a family." But José became enraged, grabbed a can of food from the kitchen counter, and struck her in the head with it. Gwen fell to the floor again, then he took a frying pan from the stove and swung it, hitting her in the head.

Emotions were raging all around. Jaron and Jason knew what was inevitably going to happen. "They're going to kill that bitch," one of them said to the other. The two left the house, went to Jason's house, and returned with a pickaxe and shovels. They knew they would have a body to dispose of.

When Jason and Jaron arrived back at the house, Gwen was still alive and conscious, but bleeding profusely from the head and sitting on the couch. Worried that she would stain the couch, José ordered her off. Michael wasn't finished with her yet, though. He grabbed her and continued beating her.

Gwen lost consciousness when Michael hit her with his knee, smashing her head against the living room wall, cracking the plaster. Jason then joined in and started kicking her while José continued crying and tried to clean the blood from the couch and carpet.

With Gwen unconscious, Michael tied her ankles and wrists with rope and wrapped her in a comforter in an attempt to stop the blood from spreading throughout the house. He then dragged her into the garage.

Jaron watched as Michael placed a rope around her neck. Michael twisted the rope around her neck. He twisted and twisted until it eventually strangled her. Jason then hit her in the head twice with a shovel. Jaron wasn't sure if the strangling or the shovel had killed her, but it was clear—Gwen was dead.

The men put her body in the back of Michael's pickup truck, smoked cigarettes, and discussed what they should do. All four men drove east throughout the night. They drove for four hours, deep into the El Dorado National Forest in the Sierra Nevada mountains. As the morning light poked over the mountains, they dug a shallow grave.

José told the others, "I'm so mad I could still kick her a couple times more." The men put her in the ground, covered her up, and had breakfast at a McDonald's on the way home.

————

It wasn't unusual for Gwen to stay out all night. But when she didn't return home on the second night, her mother called police to report her missing. Initially, police didn't take her disappearance seriously. She was transgender and was known to stay out late.

It's hard enough for two people to keep a secret, but seven people knew this secret. Keeping it that way would prove to be impossible. Within two days, Jaron Nabors was noticeably stricken with guilt. He needed to let his secret out. When a friend confronted him about his melancholy, he confessed what he and the three other men had done.

Jaron's friend went to police with the information and agreed to wear a wiretap. The friend's next conversation with Jaron was recorded; he incriminated himself and was quickly arrested. On October 15, eleven days after they buried Gwen, Jaron Nabors led police to the gravesite.

———

Michael Magidson, José Merél, and Paul Merél were initially arrested. However, when Nicole Brown and Emmanuel Merél informed police that Paul had left the house before the killing and took no part in the violence, he was released.

As Jaron sat in jail, he wrote a letter to his girlfriend. In the letter he described a "Soprano-type plan to kill the bitch and get rid of her body." Detectives, however, intercepted the letter which also implicated Jason Cazares, who at that time had only been considered a witness. Jason was subsequently arrested as well.

———

Jaron Nabors was the most willing of the four to speak to police. After four months behind bars, Jaron pleaded guilty to voluntary manslaughter. The conviction came with an eleven year prison sentence as long as he agreed to testify against the other three during their trial. If he didn't testify, the charge would be changed to murder and his sentence extended.

———

At the trial, the prosecuting attorney referred to Gwen using her birth name, Eddie. He argued that the three men had acted as a jury of their own:

"the wages of Eddie Araujo's sin of deception were death."

The defense attorney argued for a defense known as "gay panic." He claimed his clients were "shocked beyond reason" when they realized that they'd had sex with a man. He claimed that California law calls for a charge of manslaughter at most, rather than murder.

Although Jaron Nabors testified against his friends, he added that he felt that Michael and José had been raped. Araujo "didn't come clean with being what he really was. I feel like he forced them into homosexual sex, and my definition of rape was being forced into sex." When the prosecution asked him how Gwen had "forced" them, he replied, "Through deception."

After nine days of deliberation, the jury couldn't decide if the murder was premeditated. Although most of the jury wanted to convict Michael of first-degree murder, some wanted to acquit the others. Ultimately, because they could not unanimously decide, the trial ended in a mistrial.

———

The second trial began more than a year later in May 2005. By that time, Gwen's mother was granted approval to have her name posthumously changed, requiring the defense lawyers to refer to her as Gwen rather than Eddie. Also, all three defendants had the charge of hate-crime added to their first-degree murder charge.

During the second trial, all three defendants blamed each other, including Jaron Nabors. José claimed Jaron was the one that hit her in the head with the shovel, while Michael had strangled her. Michael admitted to strangling her, but also said Jaron hit her in the head.

After over three months of testimony, Michael Magidson and José Merél were both found guilty of second-degree murder and received a sentence of fifteen years to life in prison. On the hate crime charge, they were both found not-guilty.

The jury, however, was again undecided on Jason Cazares. To avoid a third trial, he agreed to plead no contest to a lesser charge of manslaughter and was sentenced to just six years in prison with credit for the time he had already done.

———

In the years after Gwen's death, her mother suffered from Post-Traumatic Stress Disorder and was unable to return to work as a legal assistant. As of 2016, she was homeless.

The murder of Gwen Araujo resulted in changes in California laws. The change limited the use of gay or trans panic as a defense; defendants may no longer claim they were provoked to murder a person based on their gender or sexual orientation.

———

By 2016. Jason Cazares, Jaron Nabors, and José Merél had all been released from prison. Michael Magidson, however, told his parole board that he was not ready to be released in 2016 and his parole was denied. In 2019 he was denied parole a second time.

CHAPTER 4
SAVING A SOUL

On a crisp October night in 1958, fifteen-year-old Carl Eder threw a rope out of his second-story bedroom window, quietly climbed down, and disappeared into the dark suburb of Rochester, New York.

Eder spent the next month hitchhiking his way across the country, eventually ending up in the San Diego area. As the child of a first-generation German immigrant family, Eder had experience making cabinetry for his father and looked for work in the area, but had trouble because of his age.

The six-foot-four boy crossed the southern border of the United States into Tijuana, Mexico, where he found a shop that would make him a fake identification card. Eder paid for his ID card, called himself "Charles Harrison", and crossed back into San Diego.

Still unable to find work, Eder slept in a coat closet in the Mission Beach Ballroom. That was when he first met thirty-nine-year-old Tom Pendergast.

———

Tom Pendergast was a religious man. As a youth, he spent time in reform school after he and some friends were caught stealing a car and taking it for a joyride. After that experience, he made it his life's mission to help young boys find their way in life and avoid a life of crime.

Throughout the years, Tom had tried to help four young boys. He brought them into his home in El Cajon, just east of San Diego, and introduced them to his wife and children. He gave them food and a place to sleep and helped them try to find work. His efforts, however, hadn't always worked. On one occasion a boy that he let into his home robbed him and was never seen again – but that didn't deter Tom. He believed God had a task for him and he was determined to follow through.

On a stormy Southern California night, Tom Pendergast was driving home from work when he saw the pimply-faced Carl Eder hitchhiking on the side of the highway. He felt sorry for the boy and knew right away that he was homeless, headed for a life of crime, and needed help. Tom offered the boy a ride and Eder introduced himself as Charles Harrison. By the end of the drive, Tom invited Eder to his family home for dinner and a place to sleep for the night.

The Pendergast family embraced Eder and were more than happy to let him stay in a cottage they had on their property while he looked for work. Lois Pendergast made dinner every night for Eder, Tom, and their four young children; Diane, Allen, Thomas Jr., and David.

Six weeks had passed and Eder still hadn't found work. During the day he sat at home while Mrs. Pendergast watched after the two youngest children and Tom worked as an aircraft mechanic. The two oldest boys were in school.

In the early afternoon of December 15, 1958, Eder was annoyed with four-year-old Diane Pendergast. She was being a typical hyper girl and wanted to play. When Eder told her it was time to take a nap, she protested as any four-year-old would. She jumped up and down on the bed, ran around the room, and screamed. But Eder had had enough. He grabbed the girl and threw her to the floor. When the small girl's head hit the hard floor, it cracked her skull. She was killed instantly.

Thirty-nine-year-old Lois Pendergast ran into the room and screamed, "You killed her! You killed her!" Eder was in a panic. He ran to the garage where he kept his suitcase, grabbed his .38 caliber pistol, and put shells in it. He then ran back into the house and shot two warning-shots into the wall. When Mrs. Pendergast screamed, he shot her in the left side of her chest. As she lay on the floor, he put the gun to her left temple and shot again.

Eder ran back into the garage, reached back into his suitcase, and removed a ten-inch hunting knife. He returned to the house to find two-year-old Allen Pendergast screaming on the floor. He took the knife and slashed his throat, then slashed the throat of Diane to make sure she was dead. Eder pulled Diane and Allen's bodies into the bathroom and piled them on top of each other. He then dragged Mrs. Pendergast's body into the bathroom and lay her next to her children.

For the next hour, Eder sat in the front bedroom of the home and waited for the two older boys to return from school. Six-year-old Thomas Jr. got home first. When he walked in the front door, Eder grabbed him, but the boy wiggled free and ran into the garage. Thomas Jr. was no match for the tall, lanky Eder. He caught Thomas in the garage bathroom, slit his throat, and disemboweled him as if he were gutting a deer.

Soon afterwards, nine-year-old David walked in the front door to find a knife at his throat. Eder quickly sliced his throat and cut his torso from his navel to his breastplate. He left the five dead bodies inside the house, walked out the front door, sat on the front steps, and waited for Tom to get home from work.

When Tom Pendergast drove up to the house, Eder didn't give him time to exit the vehicle. He pointed his pistol at him, got in the passenger side of the car, and told him to drive. For two hours, Eder forced Tom to drive randomly through the streets of San Diego without telling him what he had done to his family.

When they reached the Mission Beach area, Eder told Tom to stop at a gas station and forced him into the men's bathroom at gunpoint. He instructed Tom to take off his clothes. He had no choice but to comply. As Eder removed his own clothes and put on Tom's, Tom attacked him and wrestled the gun away from him. Tom managed to get the gun, but Eder fled out of the bathroom door and ran down the alley.

———

Tom had escaped with his life, but he had no idea the shock he was in for when he would return home. When he opened the door to his home, he first found his oldest son, David, eviscerated on the living room floor. Then he found his wife and two youngest children piled on top of each other on the bathroom floor. Tom screamed and lifted his wife's body, pulling her into the hallway. In shock and disbelief, he cradled her in his arms and cried. Lastly, he found Thomas Jr. butchered in the garage.

When police arrived Tom was crying in the front yard, still in shock, and covered in blood. He was calm enough to tell detectives about Carl Eder, who he knew as Charles Harrison.

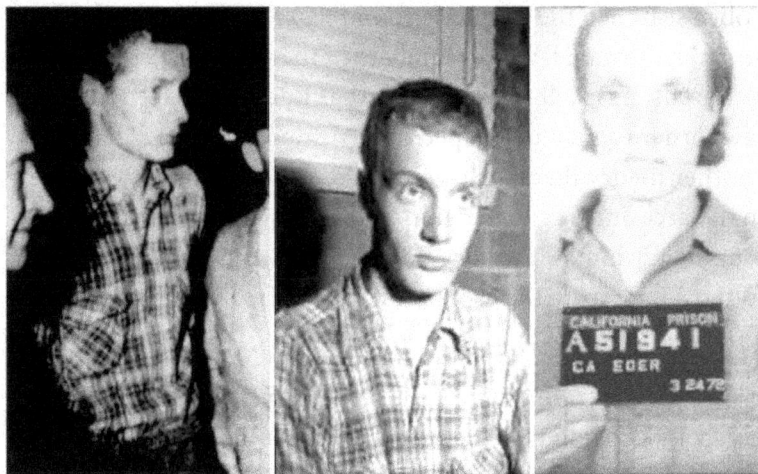

Carl Eder

Police didn't know whether or not to believe his story. Tom had the gun and it was covered in blood. His story seemed too extreme to be true, but police noticed the trousers he was wearing were far too large for him. Tom Pendergast was only five-foot-ten, while Eder was six-foot-four. Police thought there could be some truth to his story, so they alerted all law enforcement in the area and the media to be on the lookout for a suspect that matched Eder's description. They also knew that he would be wearing Tom's clothes, with trousers that would have been much too short for him.

Tom was taken to the psychiatric ward of the county hospital for fear that he may be suicidal. When doctors cleared him, he was brought to the police station where he was given multiple lie detector tests and questioned. Tom told investigators, "I was trying to save a soul" when he took Eder into his home. After seven hours of interrogation, detectives finally believed his story and stepped up the search for Carl Eder.

Police searched the canyons around San Diego on horseback and in helicopters, while members of the public called in hundreds of tips. It seemed likely that Eder may have crossed the border again and escaped into Mexico. Detectives had another theory that he may have taken another family hostage in the area and conducted hundreds of door-to-door searches looking for him. The only clue they had was his bloody t-shirt, found a mile from the gas station that he fled from.

Three days after the murders, Eder was in Mission Beach again trying to hide from authorities. He managed to buy a loaf of bread and a hamburger without being recognized, but when a man saw him walking in front of his house, he instantly recognized the short-legged pants he was wearing. The man ran next-door to his friend's house, who was a San Diego police officer.

Still wearing his pajamas, the officer hopped onto his bicycle and rode in the direction that Eder had been walking. The officer caught up with Eder at a Mission Beach amusement center that had been closed for the winter. Eder had been sleeping in the bathroom there for the past three days. When the officer confronted Eder, he claimed he didn't have any identification, but handed him a jury summons with the name Max Turner. The officer didn't believe him and said, "You are Carl Eder," to which Eder offered no resistance and said, "Yes, I am."

Tom Pendergast was at the police station when Carl Eder was arrested and brought in. Tom yelled, "Why did you do it?! Why did you do it?!" After a brief silence Eder quietly said, "I didn't want to, Tom."

When questioned by police, Eder easily admitted to killing the family, "Yes, I killed them all. The noise of the kids annoyed me. I must have flipped my lid." Eder explained how he butchered each member of the family, but when asked why he didn't kill

Tom Pendergast, he replied, "I didn't want to kill him. He was really good to me."

———

Despite being sixteen years old at the time of the murders, Eder was tried as an adult. Because he was still a juvenile, however, he was not eligible for the death penalty. Initially he pleaded innocent, but after persuasion by his lawyer he changed his plea to guilty.

At sentencing, his lawyer explained his client was eager to start psychiatric treatment, hoping that this would add some leniency to his sentence. Eder was given five life sentences, three concurrent sentences and two consecutive. He would be eligible for parole after only seven years.

As he left the courthouse, Tom Pendergast said to him, "Rest in peace there, Carl. Remember that."

Tom addressed the media and said, "I don't think he should ever be released. I don't consider him excused for killing my wife and four children because of any mental condition. He's just wicked. It was premeditated murder. Carl doesn't feel any remorse."

———

Carl Eder spent the next fifteen years moving from prison to prison throughout the California Department of Corrections. At one point he was just a few cells down from the notorious glamour girl slayer, Harvey Glatman (featured in True Crime Case Histories Volume 2).

In 1971, Eder was sent to the California Correctional Institution in Tehachapi, a minimum security prison with a population of 1,200 inmates. Tehachapi allowed him the freedom to work outside of the prison for periods of time without supervision. Eder had been working on a farm work detail for three years without incident until, one day, he vanished.

In October 1974, when he was thirty-two years old, Eder was on farm detail working completely unsupervised when he simply walked away. Personnel working at the farm didn't notice he was gone for at least seventy-five minutes.

Still wearing his prison denims, Carl Eder was on the run. When prison officials searched his cell, they found a note reading, "I've done enough time and I'm leaving."

While in prison, Eder had contact with several extremist groups including white supremacists, outlaw motorcycle groups, Venceremos Brigade, and the Symbionese Liberation Army. It's believed that any of these groups could have been involved in assisting his escape.

Throughout the years authorities tried to locate Carl Eder, including featuring him on America's Most Wanted and offering a $20,000 reward, but he seemed to have completely disappeared. There were reports he was spotted in Calistoga and St. Helena, California, but police had no luck in apprehending him. As of this time of writing, Eder would be approaching eighty years old; police speculate that he either left the country or was killed by one of his own extremist groups.

CHAPTER 5
THE JACKSONVILLE MONSTER

On a Sunday morning in 1992, thirteen-year-old Kerri Anne Buck walked toward her friend's house through her suburban neighborhood in Jacksonville, Florida, when she heard the low rumble of a vehicle pulling up behind her. Kerri Anne turned around to see a white van with tinted windows slowing down beside her.

The passenger side window of the van rolled down and the driver, a man in his thirties, called out, "Do you know Susie?" Kerri Anne replied "No" and continued walking. Slowly rolling beside her as she walked, the man then said, "Do you go to Southside Middle School?" His voice sounded angry to the young girl. She replied, "No," which was a lie.

The man was a stranger. Kerri Anne knew better than to talk to strangers. The man then stopped the van and commanded her to,

"Get the fuck in the van!"

Kerri Anne ran down the street as fast as she could. When she reached her friend's house and pounded on the door, there was no answer. She knew the neighborhood well and continued running around the corner to a large park as the man ran after her. In the park, Kerri Anne found a playground which had a children's slide shaped into a tube. She climbed the ladder, slid halfway down the tube, stopped, and wedged herself against the walls of the slide.

Kerri Anne could hear the man entering the area around the playground as she pushed harder and harder against the walls, trying not to slip out the bottom of the tube. She heard him grunt

"I know you're in there, you little bitch. I'm going to find you."

She waited for what seemed like an eternity and eventually got up the courage to peek out. He was gone. For the time being, Kerri Anne was safe. She ran back home as fast as she could.

Kerri Anne and her parents were on edge for several days afterward and Kerri was frightened to step foot outside their home. A few weeks after the incident, Kerri Anne's mother saw a strange white van parked outside their house. Mrs. Buck called her daughter to the window and Kerri Anne confirmed that it was the van of the man that tried to abduct her. Kerri's mother took down the license plate and called the police.

The owner of the van was thirty-six-year-old Donald Smith – and it wasn't his first brush with the law. Smith had been in and out of prison for sex crimes since the 1970s. As a registered sex offender, Smith was quickly arrested and sentenced to six years in prison for the attempted kidnapping of Kerri Anne Buck.

Prison was no deterrent for Smith. When he was released in the late nineties, he continued to prey on children. His obsession was insatiable. He was in and out of prison for the next fifteen years for crimes ranging from selling obscene material, voyeurism, and public masturbation, to felony child abuse.

In 2009 Smith was charged with impersonating a public employee and aggravated child abuse by willful torture. He had posed as a child welfare case worker, got a ten-year-old girl on the phone, asked her sexually explicit questions, and threatened to harm her.

After serving less than fifteen months in Jackson County Jail for the crime, the repeat sexual offender was released once again on May 31, 2013.

———

Rayne Perrywinkle had fallen on hard times – but then again, times were always hard for Rayne. Although she had given up her first-born daughter twenty years prior to relatives in Australia, she was doing her best to raise her three youngest daughters by herself in Jacksonville.

Eight-year-old Cherish Perrywinkle was the oldest of the girls living with Rayne. Rayne had had a very brief relationship with Cherish's father, Billy Jarreau. To put it bluntly, it was a one-night-stand. In 2003 she had been a stripper, Billy a recently divorced Navy officer, when they met at a Jacksonville strip club. After several nights of lap dances, Billy convinced her to go home with him. Nine months later, Cherish was born.

Initially Billy contested his paternity. He was willing to provide support for the girl, but needed proof that he was the father. Eventually a court-ordered paternity test proved he was indeed Cherish's father, so he accepted her with open arms and financial support.

Despite the financial support, Rayne continued to struggle to get her life on track. She had two more girls with another man but never married, while Billy believed Cherish would be better off living with him in California. He tried several times to get custody of the girl, but each time failed. Instead, Rayne agreed to let Cherish spend summers with her father in California.

———

On June 21, 2013, Rayne was reluctantly getting ready to send Cherish to California for the summer. The flight was scheduled for the next day and Rayne took her three girls to the Dollar General store to get Cherish some clothes for the trip. They shopped in the store for over an hour, unaware that sixty-one-year-old Donald Smith was watching them from afar.

Cherish Perrywinkle

Rayne and Cherish found a little black and white dress with hearts that they liked, but when Rayne asked the cashier the price of the dress, she realized she didn't have enough money to buy it and still pay for a taxi to the airport the next day.

Donald Smith had come into the store just minutes before and asked the cashier if they had any adult magazines. When Smith overheard Rayne explain to the cashier that she couldn't afford the dress, he took notice. He could tell that Rayne was frustrated and struggling to provide for her young girls.

When Rayne and the girls left the store, Smith approached Rayne outside of the store and said, "If you really want that dress, I'll get it for you. You look like you really have your hands full. I have a couple of little ones myself."

At first glance, he seemed harmless enough. Just an older gentleman – a good Samaritan. Rayne had no way of knowing he was a deranged predator that had been released from prison only three weeks earlier.

Smith introduced himself as Don and explained to her that he was waiting for his wife to arrive. He claimed his wife had a Walmart gift card for $150 that he was willing to give to her to help buy Cherish some clothes. Rayne was apprehensive about talking to a complete stranger, but he spoke at length about his own young children and wife—none of which existed. He told her he worked for the charity Habitat for Humanity—another lie.

When Rayne informed him that she needed to get home and get Cherish ready for her flight, he told her to be patient and encouraged her to wait. His wife would show up any minute and she would be driving a gold car. He then reached into his pocket, opened his phone, and pretended to talk to someone on the other end. After the call he said, "That was my wife. She's just going to meet us at Walmart."

Walmart was ten minutes away and Rayne didn't own a car. She had no way to get there other than by taxi, but of course, Smith offered to take them in his van. Still feeling uneasy, she declined at first, but he insisted he was no threat. "Do you want to see my driver's license or something?" He did his best to make her feel foolish for being paranoid, so eventually she accepted the ride.

When they arrived at Walmart around 9:00 p.m., Rayne and the girls entered the store while Smith faked another phone call. He then told Rayne that his wife had called and the two of them would like to take them out for dinner after shopping, but Rayne had no intention of going out to dinner with them. Her only concern was getting the gift card for her kids and going home.

Cherish tried on clothes for over an hour and a half while Rayne put the girls' items into her push cart. The only item Smith put in the cart was some rope that he picked up in the hardware department. As he watched the girls shopping, Rayne was shocked when Cherish brought a pair of women's high heel shoes to her and asked if she could try them on. She immediately told her, "No, those aren't kids' shoes! Where did you get those?" Cherish replied, "Don wanted me to try them on." Rayne told him, "Those are women's high heels! I wouldn't even wear heels that high!"

After shopping for almost two hours, Smith's wife still hadn't arrived. Each time Rayne asked where she was, he just replied that she was "on her way." At 10:30 p.m., Walmart announced that the store would be closing in thirty minutes. The girls were getting tired and hadn't had any dinner yet. Smith held his hand up next to his face imitating a sock-puppet and said to the girls, "I'm going to McDonald's. What do you want to eat?" All the girls screamed "cheeseburgers!"

Smith started walking toward the McDonald's restaurant located within the Walmart store near the front entrance and Cherish followed him. Rayne was initially concerned, but Smith had spent the entire night making Rayne feel over-protective.

She knew there were security cameras all over the store and believed there was no chance he could disappear with her daughter. Ignoring her better judgement, Rayne let her daughter follow the man she had met only hours ago.

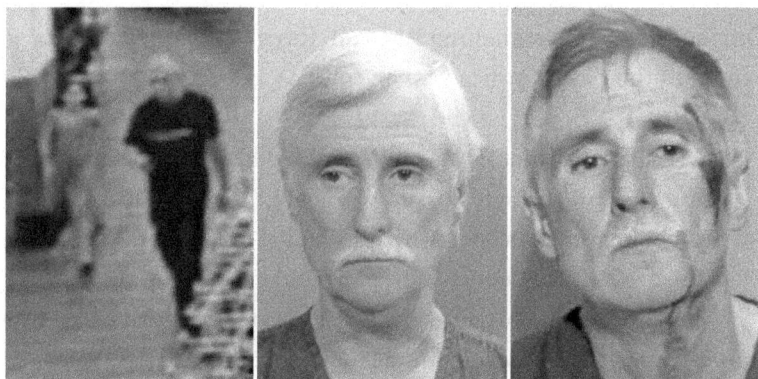

Donald Smith (Walmart security footage & mugshots)

Knowing the store was closing soon, Rayne and her two girls finished up their shopping and pushed their cart toward the front of the store. When they got to the McDonald's, Cherish and Donald Smith were nowhere to be found. Rayne pushed her cart with a quickened pace back and forth along the front of the store, looking down each aisle for her daughter. As she passed each empty aisle, she felt her heart beating harder and harder. With each step, she became more and more panicked.

When Walmart announced they were closing for the night and she couldn't find her daughter, terror overwhelmed her. Rayne was frantic and asked for help from Walmart employees, "Call 911, my daughter's been taken!" Rayne didn't have a working phone of her own and asked them to call, but the Walmart employees didn't take her seriously. The store was massive and the employees just assumed the young girl was lost.

Rayne continued to panic. She looked through the store and in the parking lot, but there was no sign of her daughter or Smith's white van. After 11:00 p.m., the store had closed and Rayne hadn't seen her daughter for a full thirty minutes before a Walmart employee finally let her borrow a cell phone.

During the heart-wrenching 911 call, Rayne explained the events of the day as police rushed to the scene:

> "... I had a bad feeling, I thought, well, I feel like pinching myself cause this is too good to be true, so I got to the checkout and he's not here and I'm hoping he's not raping her right now, cause I've had that done to me. I don't understand why he would leave right now unless he was gonna rape her and kill her - that's the only reason. And I'm wasting my time standing here!"

Rayne was so distressed she couldn't even remember what her daughter had been wearing that day. Throughout the night Rayne described the van and Smith's appearance to police. Using the description and checking the local sex offender registration, police quickly knew they were looking for Donald Smith. By 4:00 a.m., police had issued an Amber alert. By morning, the entire area of Jacksonville was looking for Cherish, Smith, and Smith's white van.

Just after 7:00 a.m., police received a call from a woman in north Jacksonville. She had seen a white van parked in an odd spot. It was discreetly parked in some bushes behind a church. It seemed suspicious to the woman because it was wedged deeply into the bushes. The woman suspected that someone in the van had dumped something in the bushes, but when police arrived and did the initial search of the area, they found nothing.

Smith lived with his mother. The police had already been to her house looking for him, but she claimed she had no idea where he was. After they left the house, police received a call from a man that rented a room at the Smith home. He told police that the prior afternoon, he had helped Smith remove the middle row of seats from his van. He also said that Smith had told him that if he ever had to run from the police, he would hide in the woods near a homeless camp in the area. Smith had told the man that he knew someone that had lived at the camp for twenty-eight years without police ever bothering him.

Every division of law enforcement in the area was on the lookout for Smith's 1998 white Dodge van. It didn't take long to find him. Before noon the morning after the abduction, Smith was pulled over and arrested… but there was no trace of Cherish. When the arresting officer noticed his pants were soaking wet, he yelled to the other officers, "Oh my God, she's in the water!"

Police rushed back to the Highlands Baptist Church. The earlier caller's suspicions were correct. The same officer that arrested Smith found the body of eight-year-old Cherish Perrywinkle wedged under a tree in a marshy wetland behind the church. Her body had been weighed down with chunks of asphalt and hidden with grass and branches. She was still wearing the bright orange dress with a fruit pattern on it, but naked beneath it. Her underwear and purple flip-flops were never found.

The sixty-seven pound girl had been gagged, raped, and sodomized for hours before she was strangled to death with a piece of clothing. The massive force of the trauma caused her gums, nostrils, and eyes to bleed. A forensic pathologist that examined Cherish's body would later tell the court, "She had so much trauma, her anatomy was totally distorted by the trauma she suffered."

———

The trial of Donald Smith didn't begin until February 2018, almost five years later. Smith faced the death penalty if found guilty. The trial was incredibly emotional as Rayne Perrywinkle recounted the horrifying evening. The jury was shown photos of the young girl that made them gasp out loud and cover their eyes. Some cried out loud. Even Smith turned his back and couldn't look at the autopsy photos of Cherish.

The Walmart and Dollar General security camera footage evidence against him left very little doubt of his guilt. When asked if the defense wanted to cross-examine Rayne, Smith said,

> "I don't want her to go through anything she doesn't have to go through. I'm done."

The jurors took only fifteen minutes to convict Donald Smith of kidnapping, rape, and murder. The week following his conviction, the jurors were asked if he should spend life in prison or be executed. New constitutional guidelines required a unanimous decision; every juror chose the death penalty.

At sentencing, Judge Mallory Cooper's voice cracked with emotion when she told Smith,

> "Donald Smith, you have not only forfeited your right to live among us, you have forfeited your right to live at all. May God have mercy on your soul."

———

After suffering the loss of her daughter, Rayne Perrywinkle's troubles were not over. The public condemned her, blaming her for leaving her daughter alone with Smith. Some went so far as to speculate that she was somehow involved in human trafficking. It didn't help matters when it came out during a deposition that Rayne claimed she was a clairvoyant and had a vision that her daughter would be dead by the time she was eight years old.

After the death of Cherish, Rayne was unable to shake the extreme grief of the traumatic event topped off with the blame from the public. She couldn't keep a job and was often turned down because everyone knew her name.

The state of Florida gave her twelve months to show that she could provide for her two remaining daughters, but it wasn't enough. Nine-year-old Destiny and seven-year-old Nevaeh were inevitably adopted by Rayne's sister and now live with their older sister, Lindsay, in Australia.

CHAPTER 6
DEAD IN THE WATER

To say life on their 300-acre dairy farm was "busy" was a gross understatement. It was exhausting. Hal and Jo Rogers spent excruciatingly long hours working their northwest Ohio farm for nearly every day of their adult lives. They were a hard-working family, to say the least.

Hal and Jo were high-school sweethearts who married just a few months after graduation and immediately started a family. Michelle was born first. Three years later came Christe.

As the years passed, they gave the girls chores on the farm such as working in the barn and looking after the cows. Christe was a daddy's girl and followed her father around the farm as often as she could. Although the young girls grew up loving life on the farm, over the years the day-in-day-out monotony and hard work wore on their mother, Jo.

Hal owned and worked the farm jointly with his younger brother, John, who lived in a small trailer on the same property. But John was a little odd. He wore military fatigues and often told tall tales of his non-existent work with the CIA and Secret Service.

In March 1988, however, John was accused of rape by a woman that lived with him in his trailer. The woman told police he wore a mask, bound her arms with handcuffs, blindfolded her, and raped her while holding a knife to her throat. Although he wore a mask, she told police she recognized his voice. She also said that he had videotaped the rape.

When detectives entered the trailer with a warrant, they found a briefcase with a videotape of the rape, just as the woman had claimed. The briefcase contained more than just the rape video, however.

Detectives found photos of Michelle, who was sixteen at the time. She was naked, blindfolded, and her hands and feet were bound with rope. They also found cassette audio tapes of Michelle screaming for John, her uncle, to let her go.

When confronted, Michelle confirmed the rape and told police that John had been raping her for more than two years. He told her he would kill her if she ever told anyone.

Before Hal knew about Michelle's accusation, he had promised his brother that he would post his $10,000 bond. But, despite posting the bond, the news destroyed the Rogers family. Hal and John's mother refused to believe her grand-daughter and stood by her son, John. This drove Hal away from his mother.

Initially, John denied the rapes. Michelle was embarrassed and traumatized and had no intention of testifying against him. She just wanted it all to go away. In the end, she didn't need to testify. John pleaded guilty to raping the first woman and was sentenced to seven to twenty-five years in prison.

With the rape of his daughter and the loss of the relationship with his mother and brother, Hal fell into a deep depression. He became despondent and would sometimes disappear for days at a time, locking himself in his brother's trailer. The small town gossip weighed on the entire family.

The following year, Jo and the girls thought it would be good to get away for a while. Hal couldn't leave the farm, but at least the three girls could get a respite from the small town. Michelle and Christe had never had a real vacation. They had never even left the state of Ohio. Even Jo had only left the state once, for her and Hal's honeymoon, to spend a night in a hotel in Fort Wayne, Indiana.

Christe, Michelle, and Jo Rogers

The three girls planned a trip to Florida, where they could leave behind the gossip, the farm, the counselors, and the detectives. They wanted to meet Mickey Mouse and go to every theme park they could think of. What they really needed was some sunshine and sand in between their toes. Although none of them even knew how to swim, they needed to feel the warm ocean waters. Just a week away would do a world of good, they thought.

Michelle's only hesitation was being away from her boyfriend, Jeff Feasby. Although they had only been dating for less than a month, she was smitten and they spoke on the phone every night. Jeff had heard rumors of Michelle's troubles with her uncle, but he didn't know details. He didn't care to know. It was her own business and she clearly didn't want to talk about it.

Although they were only leaving for a week, Michelle and Jeff's final goodbye was emotional for the young couple. They kissed on their front porch while fourteen-year-old Christe watched. Still, all three of the women were excited to get started on their journey and packed the car the night before the trip. At the break of dawn on May 26, 1989, they left Willshire, Ohio, and headed south.

The first day of driving was both exhausting, yet exciting. Jo was known for driving fast and Michelle had only recently got her driver's license, so Jo drove most of the way. The first night they stayed in a hotel just across the Georgia border, then continued on to their first stop the next day: Jacksonville, Florida.

After a day at Jacksonville Zoo, they headed inland to Silver Springs where they took a tour on a glass-bottom boat. The family was finally having a proper vacation and filled rolls of film with snapshots along the way.

After Silver Springs, they moved toward the Atlantic coast and drove down Highway 1 toward Cape Canaveral. Jo sent a post-card to Hal, while Michelle sent a postcard to Jeff. She was feeling a bit guilty for being on vacation during the week of Jeff's birthday, so she got him a trashy joke postcard – it had a bikini-clad woman rolling in the sand on the Florida beach with an alligator snapping at her bikini bottom. The postcard read:

> "Hi! How is everything with you? I'm doing great. Yesterday we went to the Zoo in Jacksonville. I was visiting my relatives, and we found Geoffrey (you). Later we went to Silver Springs and rode on a glass-bottom boat. Today we are going to a beach and

then to Sea World. You have fun at work and behave yourself. Have a great birthday. I'll be thinking of you! I miss you!

Love ya,

Chelle"

The girls had no intention of slowing down. The following days they went to Sea World, Epcot Center, and Disney's Hollywood Studios. By Thursday, they were ready to explore the bay side of Florida and headed to Tampa.

Just after noon, the three girls checked into their hotel overlooking Tampa Bay and snapped a few photos as they unpacked their suitcases. Michelle called Jeff for his birthday while Jo and Christe looked at brochures they had picked up in the hotel's lobby. The Busch Gardens brochure seemed promising. Jo called Busch Gardens for more information and wrote directions on the brochure so they could go the next day.

That evening, the three girls were seen having dinner in the hotel restaurant. However, this was the last time they were seen alive.

———

Jo and the girls were due back at the farm that Sunday, June 4. Jo was scheduled for work and Michelle's summer school started on Monday, but there was no sign of them. Hal hadn't heard a word.

———

That same Sunday morning, a sailboat was passing under the Sunshine Skyway Bridge, where Tampa Bay opens into the Gulf of Mexico. As the boat lumbered toward the gulf, the captain noticed something floating in the water. He slowed the boat and it gradually became clear that the floating object was a body.

The captain of the boat called the Coast Guard to report what they had found. It was the body of a female. She was floating face-down and naked below the waist. Both her legs and feet were bound with yellow rope. The same type of yellow rope was tying her neck to something beneath the water, partially weighing her down. The Coast Guard, however, couldn't lift the object that was tied around her neck. They cut the rope, let the object sink, and lifted the body aboard. As they headed toward the marina, another call came in. Someone had found a second body.

Not far north of the first body was another similar site. A female, face-down, bound with the same type of yellow rope and naked below the waist. A rope around her neck was tied to a large object beneath the water. Minutes after finding the second body, another call came in of a third body.

When the Coast Guard retrieved the bodies, they realized that all three had been weighed down by a large concrete block tied to the rope around their necks. The bloating caused by decomposition, however, had caused the bodies to float to the surface despite the heavy weight.

Each of the bodies had been bound in the same manner with the same type of rope, but one of the girls had managed to get a hand free. All three were also gagged, with duct tape over their mouths.

Although decomposition had made it difficult to determine with certainty if they had been sexually assaulted, the fact that they were all naked from the waist down seemed to point to that conclusion. There were no defensive wounds and no evidence that a knife or gun was used against them. However, the evidence indicated that they had been alive when they entered the water with concrete tied around their necks.

———

Although Jeff had barely known Michelle's father, he repeatedly called Hal at the farm asking if he had heard from them. Both of them were getting worried. Hal had called Jo's friends and relatives, but nobody had heard a word. By Wednesday, the girls were three days late and Hal had worked himself into a panic. He went to the bank to withdraw $7,000 in cash with a plan to hire a private plane. He thought he could search the route from Ohio to Florida from the air.

———

Although the Rogers party was due to check out of their hotel almost a week prior, the maid at the Tampa Days Inn noticed the suitcases hadn't moved from room 251. The beds had never been slept in, the soaps were still wrapped in paper, and a purse lay on the table. Each day she walked in to clean the room, but nothing had been touched.

The news of the three female bodies was on the television news in Tampa every night. On Thursday, June 8, the hotel management called the Tampa police. When detectives arrived, they thoroughly examined the room. Fingerprints lifted from a tube of toothpaste matched fingerprints from one of the bodies. Using the hotel registration, they were able to identify the female victims as the Rogers girls.

———

Hal Rogers had already been in a deep depression dealing with the rape of his daughter by his brother. When the local Sheriff told him of the rape and murder of his wife and both daughters, it was more than he could handle. Television cameras and reporters were at his door almost immediately after the news became public. He fell apart emotionally, but kept working. The farm still needed to be run.

————

Police found the Roger's car parked near the Courtney Campbell Parkway at a boat ramp just a few miles from their hotel. Nothing seemed out of the ordinary. Christe's stuffed cow toy was still stuck to the back window with suction cups. On the front seat police found a sheet from a Days Inn notepad where Jo had written directions to the boat ramp:

"turn rt (w on 60) - 2 1/2 mi - on rt side alt before bridge"

Below that was:

"blue w/wht"

It appeared that someone had given them instructions to the boat ramp. Detectives assumed they were told to look for a blue and white boat.

Also on the front seat of the car was a brochure for Clearwater Beach, Florida. Written at the bottom of the brochure were directions back to their hotel. The handwriting on the brochure, however, wasn't the same as the handwriting on the Days Inn note paper. Someone other than Jo had written it.

————

During their investigation, detectives learned of Michelle's rape by her uncle. Although John Rogers was in prison at the time, police needed to eliminate the possibility that John had somehow had something to do with the girls' death. Both incidences involved being bound with rope – had he somehow arranged to have them killed from behind bars? To find out, detectives flew to Ohio.

When detectives interviewed John Rogers in prison, they quickly realized that he had nothing to do with the murders. There was no way he could have arranged something from behind bars. Even within the prison, John was a loner and had few friends. He had no packages delivered and the only phone call or visitor to the prison had been his mother.

———

Hal Rogers was having trouble making sense of his life. The constant badgering by news crews drove him crazy. To cope, he kept working on his farm. At the funeral, he fought back the urge to punch his own mother. He couldn't believe she had the nerve to show up at her granddaughter's funeral after calling her a liar and saying she had made up the rape charge. While the entire congregation sobbed, Hal was more angry than sad. He was mad at his mother, mad at God, mad at the killer… he sat behind his tinted glasses, silently showing no emotion. After the funeral, he went straight back to working the farm.

Detectives took notice of Hal's behavior and, for a brief time, considered him a possible suspect. It seemed suspicious that he had paid his brother's $10,000 bond after his arrest. Then, just days after the murders, he made a $7,000 cash withdrawal from the bank. His actions definitely raised questions, but in the end Hal was able to account for the cash he withdrew and police confirmed he had never left the state of Ohio.

Investigators used a forensic handwriting expert to analyze the brochure they found in the Rogers' car. They knew it wasn't any of the girl's handwriting. Right away, the examiner noticed two unique characteristics about the handwriting: the person who wrote the note had a peculiar habit of capitalizing T's in the middle of words. There were also four Y's in the note, each written in a different style.

The brochure was also analyzed for fingerprints. There were several fingerprints on the brochure, but all belonged to the Rogers girls. Only one print was unidentified—a partial palm print. But until detectives had a suspect to match it to, the print was useless.

Hundreds of tips came in from the public throughout Florida, but one in particular seemed to be relevant. A twenty-four-year-old woman named Judy Blair was visiting from Canada and told police she was approached by a man just two weeks before the murders in the same area. The man offered to take her out for a sunset cruise on his blue and white boat. Once they were out in the open water and away from other boats, the man sexually assaulted her.

Judy told police he had approached her one evening at a 7-Eleven store. He was a white male in his mid-thirties with reddish-blonde hair, about 5 foot 10 and 180 pounds. She mentioned he was friendly and drove a dark color Jeep Cherokee with tinted windows.

He took her out on a sunset cruise, but once the sun had set, he tried to have sex with her. When she refused, he got angry and attacked her. He screamed at her,

"What are you doing? Nobody's going to hear you. What are you going to do? Jump out of the boat? Is sex something worth losing your life over?"

She pleaded with him, telling him that she was a virgin, but that seemed to excite him more.

Once he was finished, the man seemed to have immediate regret for his actions and apologized for what he had done.

"I've taken something from you that you can never get back,"

he told her before vomiting over the edge of the boat.

As he drove the boat toward the shore, he threw up several more times. The man took her camera, pulled the film out, and threw it overboard. When the boat reached the shoreline, he spared her life and let her swim to safety.

Judy told police that he had completely removed her shorts and bikini bottoms during the rape, just like how the Rogers girls were found. She said she noticed rope on the boat that was similar to the rope used in the murders and he had threatened to tape her mouth with duct tape.

Detectives knew this had to be the same man. Using the girl's description, police created a composite drawing of the man which was released to the public. The sketch was aired on the television news, printed in the newspapers, and used for posters distributed through the area. More and more tips poured in, but most were dead ends.

————

Over three years had passed since the murders. Investigators believed their best hope was the unique handwriting on the brochure that was left in the car. Maybe if they released it to the public, someone would recognize it. Police placed five billboards throughout the Tampa area near the boat ramp. The billboards featured a large image of the handwriting and asked the question "Who wrote these directions?" It was a long-shot, but they hoped for the best.

————

The day after the billboards went up, Jo Ann Steffey did a double-take. Her heart skipped a beat when she realized that she knew the handwriting. She had just seen the composite sketch of the suspect in that morning's paper and rushed home to look again.

The description of the suspect seemed to match a neighbor that lived just two doors down. Forty-three-year-old Oba Chandler was an aluminum siding contractor that had done some work on her house. He was married and had eight children from seven different women. As she read the story in the paper, everything seemed to fit together.

His reddish-blond hair fit the description, as did his size and weight. He resembled the composite sketch. He drove a dark blue Jeep Cherokee and his house backed onto a canal where he had his own boat. A blue and white boat. The canal he lived on led to the bay, just a mile from the boat ramp.

Jo Ann then remembered that she still had the invoice Chandler had written for the work he had done. When she looked at the handwriting on the invoice, she noticed right away that he had the habit of capitalizing his T's in the middle of a word. She immediately called police.

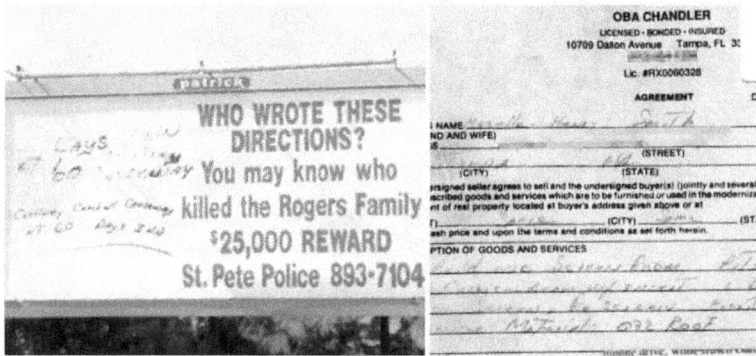

Billboard and matching handwriting

Oba Chandler was born in 1946 and had grown up in Cincinnati, Ohio. When he was five years old, one of his brothers died. His father never recovered from the loss. Five years later, his father hanged himself in the basement of their home. According to one of his cousins, Oba jumped into the grave as the gravediggers shoveled the dirt over the coffin. He stomped the dirt with each shovel full.

In his early teenage years, Oba was arrested for stealing cars. By the time he reached eighteen, he had been arrested twenty times. Throughout his adult life, he constantly found trouble. He had been charged with loitering, burglary, possession of counterfeit currency, armed robbery, and kidnapping. In one instance, he was caught masturbating as he looked through the ground-floor window of a woman's home. On another occasion, he and an accomplice robbed a Florida couple's home. He tied the man up and made the woman take off her clothes. He tormented her by slowly rubbing his gun across her naked stomach.

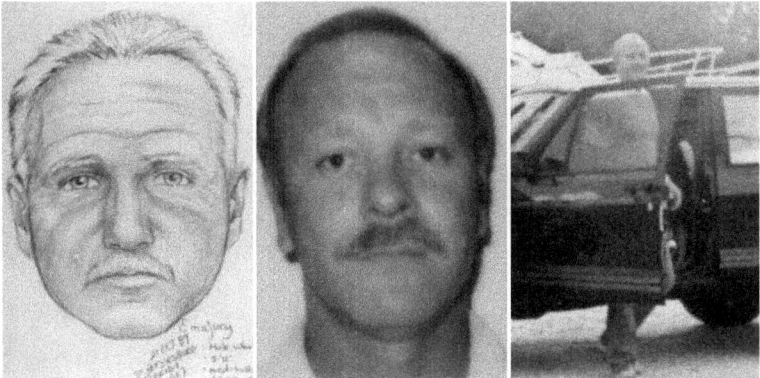

Police sketch and Oba Chandler with Jeep Cherokee

Oba Chandler was arrested on September 24, 1992. When placed in a police lineup, without hesitation Judy Blair identified him as the man that had raped her. Additional samples of his handwriting were analyzed and matched the handwriting on the brochure exactly. The palm print on the brochure also matched his left palm print.

While building the case against Chandler, detectives gathered ship-to-shore phone records from the night of the rape and the night of the murders. On both occasions he placed phone calls to his wife that put him in the location of the crimes during the times that they happened.

At trial, Oba Chandler was advised by his lawyer to not testify in his defense, but he did so anyway. He insisted that he met the Rogers girls, gave them directions, and never saw them again except in the newspapers and the billboards. He claimed that he was in his boat on Tampa Bay those nights, but he was fishing by himself. He said he had engine trouble with his boat, asked the Coast Guard for help, but ended up fixing the problem himself.

During the trial, Judy Blair flew down from Canada to testify that Chandler had raped her on his boat just two weeks before the Rogers murders. A former employee of Chandler's testified that the morning after the murders, Chandler boasted that he "dated" three women on the bay the night before.

Two of Chandler's daughters and his son-in-law all testified against him. His daughter, Kristal Sue Mays, told the court that while he was visiting family in Ohio just after the murders, she overheard her father saying, "I can't go back to Florida because police are looking for me because I killed some women." She continued, telling the court that her father had also told her that he had raped a woman near Madeira Beach, Florida.

Two of Chandler's cell mates from jail also testified against him. One claimed that Chandler said, "I'm not the only one that ever uses duct tape, but it's easy to tie someone up with." The second told the court that Chandler said, "If the bitch didn't resist, I wouldn't be here in jail."

Oba Chandler was found guilty of all three murders and was sentenced to death on November 4, 1994. At his sentencing, Judge Susan F. Schaeffer told him,

> "Oba Chandler, you have not only forfeited your right to live among us under the laws of the state of Florida. You have forfeited your right to live at all. Mr. Chandler, may God have mercy on your soul."

In an interview, Judge Schaeffer later described Chandler as

> "A man with no soul. It's the worst case, as far as a defendant without saving grace, that I ever handled. And I represented plenty of people who were not necessarily good people."

Since he was already on death row for the murders, prosecutors spared Judy Blair the emotional heartache of going through a rape trial.

Although he was suspected of several more similar murders, no additional charges were ever brought against him. On November 15, 2011, Oba Chandler was executed. His last words were

"Kiss my rosy red ass."

His written statement wrote:

"Oba Chandler LasT StatemenT

You are killing a innocent man Today

Nov. 15th 2011

Oba Chandler"

He had capitalized every T.

Three years after his execution, DNA evidence proved that Oba Chandler had murdered twenty-year-old Ivelisse Berrios-Beguerisse. Her body was found in Coral Springs, Florida, in 1990. Chandler lived just a mile away at the time.

CHAPTER 7
THE CARNIVAL CULT

In the early nineties, police in Johnson County, Indiana, noticed a surge of graffiti on walls and abandoned barns in the rural area. The vandalism seemed to be concentrated in the area around Whiteland, a small town of about 2,500 people.

Police were familiar with the symbols spray painted on the walls: pentagrams, upside down crosses, the numbers "666", and the letters "COS." The symbols were satanic. "COS" referred to the Church of Satan, while 666 referenced the "Number of the Beast" from the book of Revelations in the Bible.

The spray paint was a nuisance, but the police believed it was just the work of harmless kids. Many of the local kids were into heavy metal music, which used macabre theatrics and many of the same satanic symbols. However, police soon realized that the kids creating this graffiti were anything but harmless.

———

As a young teen, Mark Goodwin was a heavy metal kid. His favorite artist was Ozzy Osbourne, the former singer of the band Black Sabbath. Like thousands of other kids, the dark lyrics and eerie symbolism of the records he listened to intrigued Mark. Although the music was mostly dramatization, these records were his first introduction into what would become an obsession. For a seventh-grade school assignment, Mark was required to write a report on the meaning of Halloween. He checked out books about Satanism and the occult from the library, discovered *"The Satanic Bible"* by Anton LaVey, and wrote his report about demons and spirits. By the time he was fifteen, Goodwin was obsessed with Satanism and had started his own satanic cult he called "Satan's Disciples."

Satan's Disciples consisted of six or so like-minded kids in the Whiteland and Franklin area of central Indiana. At first, their meetings would consist of reading passages and chants from various satanic books and walking through graveyards late at night. Over time, however, the group were butchering small animals as a sacrifice to their lord Satan.

While many of the members were only part of the cult as an excuse to rebel against their parents and drink alcohol, Goodwin took it seriously. He wore a black robe and stayed sober as he killed the small animals. He drained the blood into a small chalice and drank from it, passing it around for everyone to sip. Afterwards they would play music, smoke pot, and dance like they were possessed. There were rumors that they would sometimes have both heterosexual and homosexual orgies.

Goodwin had his limits, however. When one member of his cult suggested they kill a baby as a sacrifice, that was too much. At eighteen years old, he walked away from the cult he had created, but his interest in Satanism never waned. He was still obsessed and read everything he could find on Satanism and the occult. Two years later, he met Keith and David Lawrence while working at a fast-food restaurant.

———

At eighteen years old, Keith Lawrence was three years younger than his brother David, yet the dominant sibling. Like Goodwin, Keith started listening to heavy metal music at an early age and listened to every word carefully. To Keith, every album became like a Bible to him. He read the same books on Satanism that Goodwin read. Around his neck he wore an upside-down cross necklace and a pentagram medallion with a goat's head, all symbols of Satanism.

Keith had been a troubled kid and a bully his entire life. In the eighth grade, his teachers recommended psychotherapy. As a result, Keith's parents sent him to boarding school - but that experience only seemed to strengthen his hatred of all people. It was during those years that he found Satanism.

The older brother, David Lawrence, wasn't as intrigued by Satanism. Keith, however, intimidated his older brother, bullying him into giving his life to Satan. In one instance, Keith chased his brother through the house with a knife, threatening to kill him if he didn't become a Satanist. David, however, didn't get along with the other members of his family. He respected his little brother and spent most of his time with him, regardless of his beliefs.

———

Mark Goodwin and Keith Lawrence had a lot in common; Keith's views on Satanism intrigued Mark. The young men became inseparable and eventually Mark and Keith drew up a twenty-year written contract devoting their lives to Satan. They both signed it in their own blood. Each believed the contract would provide them with anything they wanted for the next twenty years. "After twenty years are up, Satan can do what he wants or kill us. At the time we really didn't care," Goodwin later recalled.

In May 1991, all three boys had troubles with home life and were days away from being thrown out by their parents. David suggested they all work as carnival workers with a company that travelled throughout Ohio and Indiana during the summer for local county fairs and carnivals.

The Lawrence brothers had worked for a similar amusement company the previous winter in the Bahamas. When they crossed back into the United States that January, US Customs noted that Keith had seventeen books on Satanism, witchcraft, and the occult.

The three young men got jobs as traveling carnival workers, also known as "carnies." While traveling throughout Indiana that summer, they met another worker named Jimmie Lee Penick while working in Brownstown. Twenty-four-year-old Penick fit right in with the other three. He was also a practicing Satanist.

The four men were outspoken about their involvement in Satanism and openly spoke to other carnival workers about random crimes that they had committed throughout their lives. It was okay for them to talk about their own crimes, but when eighteen-year-old Andrew Wright repeated a story he had heard about a crime that Penick had committed in Ohio, Penick became enraged.

Just east of Toledo, Ohio, on August 30, 1991, the day before the start of the Fulton County Fair, Penick and Keith Lawrence stabbed Wright to death. They slit his neck and dumped his body in the woods off of the Ohio Turnpike near Wauseon, Ohio.

Even after killing Wright, Penick and Keith couldn't help but brag about their killing and told David and Goodwin what they had done. Four people knew about the murder, so the chance of it remaining a secret was slim.

During September 1991, the four men were working at the Dekalb County Free Fall Fair when they befriended another worker named Tony Ault. Twenty-one-year-old Ault had dabbled in Satanism as well and wanted to be a part of their cult. Eventually, one of them told Ault of the murder of Andrew Wright and asked if he still wanted to be involved. Ault was undeterred. He wanted to belong.

After the carnival closed on September 25, they told Tony Ault that they were going to have a satanic ritual that night and he was welcome to come along. Goodwin's girlfriend, Brenda Ferguson, drove the five young men out to an abandoned barn deep in the woods. She dropped them off and was told to come back later to pick them up.

Outside the barn, the five men built a large bonfire. Inside the barn, Keith asked Ault to lie down on an old unhinged door as part of an initiation ritual. The door was to be used as an altar. They tied Ault to the door and put a gag in his mouth. Once he was secure, Keith began reading a chant he believed could invoke Satan.

Penick then took Keith Lawrence's knife and made a deep cut, from Ault's neck to his pelvis. The cut was just deep enough not to kill him. Goodwin and the two Lawrence brothers then made additional cuts on his torso to make the shape of an inverted cross and several other satanic symbols. They then tried to cut his ear off before Goodwin attempted to cut out his heart while it was still beating.

With Ault still strapped to the door and clinging to life, Penick took the knife again, put his face to Ault's face, and asked, "Are you ready to die?" He then slit his throat from ear to ear as Keith chanted.

The four men had no intention of allowing Ault into their cult. Instead, they wanted to ensure he didn't tell anyone about the previous murder of Andrew Wright.

Penick, Goodwin, and Keith then cut off Ault's head and hands while David watched. Keith threw his head and hands on the bonfire. This dismemberment and burning of his hands was an attempt to thwart identity. Keith, however, said he cut off and burned his head because he wanted to come back later and collect the skull to give to a friend.

When Brenda Ferguson returned to pick them up, they took Ault's money from his wallet and used it to buy a meal at Arby's.

———

The four continued to work for the carnival company through the end of the season into late October. When their jobs ended at the end of the season, Penick returned to his parent's home in Shelbyville, Indiana. Goodwin and the Lawrence brothers drove to Florida in Goodwin's van, which he had nicknamed "Rigor Mortis," where they hoped to work the winter carnival circuit.

While working in Florida, Goodwin felt guilty for what he had done and called his father back in Indiana. He explained to his father that he had witnessed a murder in Dekalb County. Goodwin assumed his father wouldn't tell the police, but on December 12, that's exactly what he did. Police questioned Goodwin's ex-girlfriend, Brenda Ferguson, who led them to the barn where she had dropped off the five men. There, detectives found the decomposed remains of Tony Ault.

Goodwin returned to Indiana on December 13 and was immediately arrested and charged with conspiracy to commit
murder. Penick was simultaneously arrested in Shelbyville on
murder charges.

The Lawrence brothers had been working in the Bahamas again
with the carnival and had no idea that Goodwin and Penick had
been arrested. When they returned to the United States on
January 10, 1992, their plane landed in Miami, Florida. US
Customs agents arrested the brothers at the border and
returned them to Indiana.

———

David Lawrence was both the first to show signs of remorse
and the first to plead guilty. He was only charged with assisting
a criminal. David insisted that he was never really a Satanist,
but was intimidated by his brother into following his lead. In
April 1993, David Lawrence was sentenced to eight years in
prison.

At his sentencing, the judge commented,

> "Although the older of the two brothers, David Lawrence was
> led and manipulated by Keith. David, in your sentence there's a
> good deal of punishment, but there's also a good deal of reha-
> bilitation. In the end, it's up to you how to deal with this. I want
> you to be a law-abiding citizen, a good husband, and a good
> father. I think you can do it."

David's brother, Keith, was sentenced the same day. Keith,
however, had been a much more active participant in the
murder and his history of prior criminal activity was well docu-
mented. Keith was initially charged with murder and faced
eighty years in prison. Eventually, he and his defense made a

deal with prosecutors to have the charge dropped to conspiracy to commit murder if he agreed to a guilty plea.

At sentencing, Keith's lawyer argued,

"No question Keith used poor judgement in picking Jimmie Lee Penick as an acquaintance. Not a friend, an acquaintance. Keith is a person who studied religions. Not a person involved in religions himself."

His lawyer went on to claim that Keith was not solely interested in the occult, but also studied the Greek and Hebrew versions of the Bible, as well as the Quran. His plan, however, failed to impress the judge. Keith was sentenced to thirty years in prison plus twenty additional years of probation. The sentence was the maximum allowed with a guilty plea.

The judge said of Keith,

"In his home community of Whiteland, Indiana, Keith had a reputation as an intimidating and dangerous character. Although Keith Lawrence did not inflict the fatal wound on Ault, he did carve an inverted cross onto the victim's torso. To sentence Keith Lawrence to less than the maximum would depreciate the seriousness of the crime."

Mark Goodwin, too, was deeply remorseful for his role in the ritualistic murder. He pleaded guilty to assisting a criminal and battery by means of a deadly weapon, but pleaded not-guilty to the charge of helping to conceal a body. As he awaited trial, he spoke to the press about the dangers of Satanism and met with a chaplain on a daily basis.

At sentencing, Mark Goodwin told Tony Ault's mother, "Mrs. Givens, I never really knew your son. Whatever I know, I do know he was a good-hearted person. I am shameful of what I did to your son." Mrs. Givens had anything but sympathy for the twenty-year-old Goodwin and cried, "You damn well should be. What chance does he have now? What am I supposed to feel... sorry for you? What? You should've never done it!" Goodwin was sentenced to eight years in prison.

In January 1994, Jimmie Lee Penick faced the death penalty in Indiana for the murder of Tony Ault. He also faced life in prison in Ohio for the murder of Andrew Wright.

To avoid the death penalty in Indiana, Penick pleaded guilty to murder. The maximum allowed for a guilty plea of murder in Indiana was sixty years, which was exactly what he got. The sentence, however, was to be served consecutively to the Ohio sentence, for which he was given twenty years to life. As of this time of writing, Jimmie Lee Penick is still serving his twenty years to life sentence in Warren Correctional Institution in Ohio. If he is ever released from the Ohio facility, he'll go straight to Indiana to start his sixty year sentence.

———

Mark Goodwin and David Lawrence each fulfilled their eight-year sentence long ago. Keith Lawrence served only eleven years of his thirty-year sentence. His original sentence included the first five years of probation to be on home detention, but upon his release the home detention was erased. While in prison, Keith Lawrence acquired a significant amount of good-time credit for earning two college degrees.

Keith Lawrence was arrested in 2006 for public intoxication, battery, and criminal confinement which violated his parole. The criminal confinement and battery charges were dropped, but the public intoxication charge remained, which landed him in jail for 180 days.

CHAPTER 8
THE MOUSSE CAN KILLER

Robert Mark Edwards didn't stand a chance in life. Born in 1961, his father didn't believe that Robert was his child and began beating him daily when he was just six months old. His abuse wasn't just directed at Robert, however—he beat Robert's brother, sister, and mother as well. His father's nickname for Robert and his brother William were "SFB1" and "SFB2" — Shit for brains 1 and 2.

Robert's father worked as a bartender and his mother was a nurse. Both were alcoholics and by the time he was eleven, his mother had a drug problem. She was addicted to Valium.

The family lived in Florida and moved briefly to Puerto Rico. When he was thirteen years old, Robert's mother finally divorced his father and moved the family to California. Shortly after their arrival in California, she was run over by a car while on a drug and alcohol binge. She lived, but her drug and alcohol habits eventually rubbed off on the kids.

Just a year after their arrival in California, Robert and his brother began breaking into homes and stealing items to pay for their own drugs and alcohol. They drank, smoked pot and hashish, and took LSD, cocaine, peyote, methamphetamines, barbiturates, heroin, and anything else they could get their hands on. His sister, Elena, wasn't immune and developed an addiction to Valium. Even both of Robert's grandmothers were addicts, one to Lorazepam and the other to Valium and oxycodone.

Robert dropped out of school in the eighth grade and soon after started selling fake LSD to kids in Long Beach, California. He and his brother sold little tabs of paper with designs on it, claiming it was LSD, but it was nothing more than printed paper.

Robert's alcohol abuse became a serious problem when he experienced his first alcoholic blackout at sixteen. He drank so much and took so many drugs that he found himself wandering the streets of Long Beach the next morning with no idea how he got there. On one occasion, he woke up under a kitchen table in a house he wasn't familiar with and had no recollection of anything from the previous night.

In March 1986, Robert met Kathryn Deeble while he was selling fake LSD near a Long Beach bus stop. He had crashed his motorcycle a few months earlier and his leg was in a cast. As Kathryn drove by the bus stop in her pickup truck, she saw Robert, felt sorry for him hobbling around in his cast, and offered him a ride. From that point on, they were a couple. Kathryn invited him into her life and introduced him to her mother, Marjorie Deeble.

Fifty-five-year-old Marjorie was a strong-willed woman. She had been a successful real estate agent living in nearby Los Alamitos, California, just inland from Long Beach. One afternoon while her mother was at work, Kathryn brought Robert to her mother's apartment. Robert took note as Kathryn retrieved a key hidden in a nearby drain pipe to get into the condo. The couple then went inside to have sex.

Kathryn and Robert had been dating for two months when she and her mother took a trip to Palm Springs together in early May. Robert helped them load their suitcases into their car and he borrowed Kathryn's truck while they were away.

The alternator in the truck, however, failed while they were gone and Marjorie blamed Robert for the problem. She became upset with Robert and demanded that he get the truck fixed before they returned. Robert agreed and took the truck to the dealer, but later it became clear that he harbored some resentment at Marjorie's harsh words towards him.

Kathryn and Marjorie returned from their trip on the morning of Monday, May 12. Kathryn dropped her mother off at her apartment and headed home. That would be the last time she saw her mother alive.

The morning of May 13, Kathryn noticed something strange. She normally parked her truck in the driveway with her driver's side door either before or after the juniper bushes so she could open the door without hitting them. That morning, however, it was parked with the door directly against the bushes, causing her to stand in the bushes as she got in.

Kathryn knew that the only other person that had access to her truck was Robert. Although she thought it was strange that he had borrowed the truck in the middle of the night, she thought little of it at the time.

Three days later, Marjorie's co-workers at Great Western Real Estate were getting worried. The sparky, petite woman that had won Salesperson of the Year in 1985 hadn't been to the office in days. That was completely out of character for her, so they called Los Alamitos Police.

The afternoon of May 16, police arrived at Marjorie's apartment for a welfare check only to find her front door cracked open. They could hear loud music playing in the bedroom, so knocked and called her name but got no answer. When they entered her bedroom, they found Marjorie Deeble dead, face-down on the floor.

She was naked from the waist down and her nightgown had been torn and pushed up to her torso. Her hands were tied behind her back with a piece of her nightgown and a telephone cord. A thin belt was tightened around her neck and the end of the belt was tied to the handle of the dresser, suspending her neck eight inches above the floor. Her legs showed signs that they had been tied at one time as well.

The bedroom was covered with blood. Drawers were open, her jewelry was missing, clothes were thrown all over, and the telephone had been ripped from the wall. A bloody pillowcase had been used as a hood over her head. Marjorie had lost a lot of blood from her ears, mouth, and nose. Her nose was broken and her face had the residue of an adhesive, indicating that she had been gagged. She had been beaten, raped, and strangled. On the bed was a bloody can of hair styling mousse that had been used to sexually assault her.

———

Robert was with Kathryn when the Los Alamitos Police called her into the station. He sat in the waiting room and could hear her crying in a nearby room when they told her that her mother had been brutally murdered.

During Kathryn's grief, Robert continued to date her for a few more weeks, but eventually they drifted away and lost contact.

The police, however, considered him a potential suspect. They asked him for a DNA sample, but he refused.

Seven years went by with no leads in the case of Marjorie Deeble's murder, but Los Alamitos Police Detectives kept track of Robert's every move. Although they had no physical evidence linking him to the murder, they patiently waited, knowing he would eventually slip up.

During the years following the murder, Edwards couldn't seem to stay out of trouble. He had been arrested in 1984 for vehicle burglary, again in 1987 on a weapons charge, and in 1988 for receiving stolen property and vehicle theft. In 1992 he moved to Hawaii and was again arrested in 1994 for kidnapping, sexual assault, robbery, and burglary.

————

In the summer of 1996, Robert Edwards was working as a roofer in the south Maui town of Kihei. He lived just a block from the beach with his girlfriend, Janice Hunt, and her twelve-year-old daughter. From the window of their second-story apartment on Kanoe Street, Janice could watch whales breaching using a pair of binoculars that she kept on a table below the window. Edwards, however, was more interested in using the binoculars to watch the neighbors.

————

Peggy Ventura was from Alaska and spent a few months every year vacationing in south Maui with her mother, sixty-seven-year-old Muriel Delbecq, a successful real estate agent. Peggy rented a condo about a half mile from the beach, while Muriel rented a ground-floor apartment on Kanoe Street, just one block from the beach—and directly across the street from Robert Edwards.

On January 25, 1993, after an evening out, Peggy dropped her mother off at her apartment and drove home. Across the street, Robert Edwards had just learned that his dog had been hit by a car. Robert sobbed and cradled the dog in his arms, but it was too late. Just a month earlier, he had learned that his step-father had been killed in a plane crash. He'd spent the past month numbing his pain with excessive alcohol and cocaine. The sudden death of his dog compounded his sorrow.

That night, Robert carried his dog's body to his kayak and paddled out into the ocean for a burial at sea. When he returned to shore around 11:00 p.m., he went to a friend's apartment, injected a half a gram of cocaine, and drank himself into a blackout.

The next morning, Janice Hunt woke to a commotion on the street outside. Police cars had gathered at the Kanoe Apartments across the street from their apartment. She walked outside and spoke to neighbors who informed her that a murder had occurred during the night.

———

At 7:30 that morning, Peggy Ventura went to her mother's apartment so they could go to the beach together for their morning walk. When she knocked on her door, however, there was no answer. A pair of flip-flops that she didn't recognize sat outside the front door. Using a key that she knew her mother had hid under a rock, she entered the apartment and immediately noticed blood on the floor. In a panic, Peggy tried to open the door to her mother's bedroom, only to find it locked. She reached for the phone in the kitchen, but it had been ripped from the wall.

Peggy ran outside to a neighbor's apartment, screamed for them to call the police, and ran to the side of the apartment to try to get in through the window. When she crawled through the window, she couldn't see. A comforter covered the window, leaving the room pitch black. In the dark, Peggy found her way to the bedroom door and opened it to let light into the room.

She could see the bedroom had been ransacked and there was more blood on the floor and walls. Beneath a pile of blankets in the middle of the bed was her mother. Muriel laid face-up, completely naked, bruised, bloody, and lifeless. She had been beaten viciously about the head, sexually assaulted and strangled to death.

When police arrived, there was evidence that Muriel's arms and legs had been bound at one time, but whatever the killer had used to bind her was gone. Her wedding ring was missing from her ring finger and other items were missing from the apartment.

Her body was sprawled on the bed with her legs open and a mousse can was still inserted into her vagina. The medical examiner said the mousse can had been inserted into both her vagina and her anus. It had been inserted so far that it protruded into her abdominal cavity. Her breasts were cut and bruised and her pubic hair had been cut or shaved off.

The killer had left behind plenty of evidence. On the wall near the bed was a bloody palm print. A white t-shirt on the floor had a bloody foot impression. There were cigarette butts on the floor and the killer had spit into the bathtub.

A bent window screen told investigators that the killer had most-likely come in through the window and unsuccessfully tried to replace it. On the windowsill and the floor near the window were pieces of dried grass that the killer had left behind.

In a dumpster near the crime scene, police found a bloody pillowcase that matched the pattern of Muriel's bedding. Inside the pillowcase was her checkbook, traveler's checks, two telephones, and two pieces of telephone cord tied together. It was obvious that the cords were used to bind her wrists and ankles. They also found a bra with the tips of the cup cut out, a pair of panties that were cut open, and several random household items from her apartment.

———

When Janice Hunt was interviewed by police, she reported that when she told Robert Edward of the murder across the street, he seemed genuinely surprised. She also claimed, however, that while they were dating Edwards liked to tie her up and had twice tried to sodomize her with a bottle. Detectives also learned that, using the binoculars near the window in their apartment, Edwards had a clear view to the front door of Muriel's apartment.

Robert Mark Edwards

It wasn't hard to tie Edwards to the crime. The bloody palm print was a match for his palm and the glob of spit in the bathtub contained his DNA. When Maui police pulled his California police record, it was nine pages long and he had been wanted in California for the past eighteen months for parole violation. When Los Alamitos detectives heard of Edward's arrest, they knew they could now link him to the murder of Marjorie Deeble as well.

At trial, Edwards blamed his frequent alcoholic blackouts. He told the court, "It's hard for me to understand that I could do something so horrible." Blackouts were, of course, no excuse for such a heinous murder. After only two hours of deliberation, a jury found him guilty. Maui county court sentenced him to five life terms plus twenty years.

Edwards was then transferred to California where, if convicted, he faced a possible death sentence for the murder of Marjorie Deeble. The two murders had astonishing similarities. Both women were near the same age, both were real estate agents who lived alone in a ground-floor apartment, both had their limbs bound with telephone cords, were strangled, and were violated with a mousse can. They even coincidentally shared the same three initials—M.E.D.

In California, Edwards didn't deny that he murdered Marjorie Deeble, but claimed he had no memory of the event. He was again found guilty of first degree murder, but the jury was deadlocked during sentencing.

His lawyers argued that his struggles with drugs and alcohol, along with the abuse by his father, contributed to his crimes. However, prosecutors pointed out the excessive nature of how the victims were tortured and mutilated before death. The second jury was unsympathetic and, on September 9, 1998, Edwards was sentenced to death.

Due to a moratorium on the death penalty in California, Edwards has spent more than twenty years on death row and, as of this time of writing, resides at San Quentin prison north of San Francisco. He writes poetry and short stories. The following is a short story by Robert Edwards.

———

As I stepped off the bus at 3:45 a.m., the cold, wet coastal air stung my face.

I inhaled deeply. Freedom! For years, I'd yearned to smell the sea air of my home city.

There was nothing open but a twenty-four-hour restaurant a mile down the road. I had no money. The manila envelope in my hand held all my worldly possessions. Tucking the envelope under my arm and thrusting my hands deep into my pockets to keep them warm, I started walking. Maybe I could wait out a night in the restaurant's foyer before being run away as a vagrant.

By the time I got there, my clothes were damp with dew, and I sat shivering on the bench in the entryway. I thought of what the morning would bring. Would my ex-wife let me see my son? Would I get any support from my family? Should I go find my old crew? No, I thought, that's what got me sent up in the first place. It wasn't going to be easy, but this time I would try to make it on my own.

The waitress inside the restaurant kept looking at me through the inner door. Finally, she opened it. I felt sure I was about to be booted out, but instead she smiled politely and said, "Sir, there's a gentleman inside who says that, if you'd like some breakfast, he's buying."

I was instantly suspicious. But it was also an opportunity to stay inside until sunrise. "Sure," I said, and I stood and followed her to the booth where the man was sitting.

I took a seat across from him, and he smiled and shook my hand. While the waitress went to get my coffee, I said, "Look, dude, I'm gonna tell you right now, if you're looking for some action, you're looking in the wrong place. I don't play that shit."

He chuckled softly and said, "I'm not sure what you're talking about, but I don't want anything. I saw you walk by the window all hunched over, and when you didn't come in, I figured you could use some grub, or coffee, at least. Order anything you want. No strings attached, OK? My name's Steve."

Reaching out to shake his hand again, I said, "I'm Rob."

Then I took the menu and ordered an especially large breakfast, so that, if he left, I'd still have some food on the table and be able to stay until I finished.

I noticed the faded US Marine Corps tattoo on Steve's forearm and asked if he'd been in long. It turned out he'd served in

Vietnam at the same time as my father. We talked about our children. Finally I admitted that I'd just got back into town after doing some time, and everything I owned was on my back or in the envelope on the table.

"Listen," Steve said, "why don't you let me get you a room for a couple of days?"

"No way," I said. Why was this guy doing this? "Whats your trip?" I asked him.

"There was a time when I was in a situation like yours," Steve said, "and someone helped me out. I wanted to pay him back, but all he said to me was 'if sometime in the future you can help someone who is down and out, then do it.' Simple as that."

I was moved by Steve's story, but I didn't take the room he offered. That was twenty-two years ago. I never got my son back. Life on its own terms proved too much for me. I'm back in prison, this time on Death Row.

CHAPTER 9
A GLITZY COWBOY TALE

Benny Binion was born in 1904, just north of Dallas, Texas. As a young boy, he traveled with his father, a horse trader, to county fairs throughout Texas rather than attending school. It was during these early years with his father that Benny learned to gamble. Although he didn't know how to read or write, Benny knew numbers. Despite it being illegal, he played poker with the farmers with whom his father did business.

In 1920, the sale of alcohol in the United States had been banned, beginning the thirteen year Prohibition Era. But Benny saw an opportunity. At just eighteen years old, he began distilling his own illegal "moonshine." He sold his spirits throughout the Dallas area, which landed him in jail a few times but didn't slow his pace.

At twenty-four years old he combined the sale of his alcohol with illegal gambling. He ran a no-limit craps game in the back room of a downtown Dallas hotel, where he catered to big spenders who had made their money with the Texas oil boom. With the odds in his favor and the local Sheriff in his back pocket, Benny made a fortune.

Benny was very unforgiving and had killed two men that crossed him by the time he was thirty-three. The first was a rum-runner named Frank Bolding. Bolding had tried to attack Benny with a knife, but Benny rolled backwards over a crate and came up shooting. His style of shooting earned him the nickname "Cowboy." The second man he killed was Ben Frieden, who ran a rival gambling hall. Benny ambushed him while he sat in a parked car and shot him three times in the heart. Although Benny was convicted of the first murder, he only served a two-year suspended sentence. When he killed Frieden, however, he purposely shot himself in the shoulder and claimed that he had acted in self-defense.

Over time, Benny acquired opposing gambling rackets from other mobsters that mysteriously died. The FBI suspected Benny of killing several other mobsters, but could never prove it. However, when the Dallas County Sheriff that had been helping him was voted out of office, Benny lost his government help. At the same time, World War II had ended and the Chicago mob had moved into the Dallas area. Benny Binion took his wife, two sons, and three daughters to Las Vegas to start his next empire.

In 1951, Benny Binion opened Binion's Horseshoe Casino on Fremont Street in Las Vegas and changed the face of gambling. His was the first casino to install carpeting on the casino floors instead of sawdust-covered wood. He offered high limits in his casino, which attracted the high rollers. His casino was the first to offer free drinks to players, $2 steaks, and give complimentary hotel rooms to high rollers.

Benny redefined Las Vegas casinos, but after only a few years in business, he was convicted of tax evasion and sold the majority of the Horseshoe. It took eleven years for the Binion family to regain control of the casino, but with his conviction Benny was no longer allowed to hold a gaming license. His five children took over the casino, one of which was his son, Ted Binion, who took the role of Casino Manager.

Ted Binion became the new face of the Horseshoe Casino for the next thirty years. Like his father, Ted considered himself a cowboy. As a boy he had spent his summers on the family's 85,000 acre ranch in Montana working with the ranch hands.

Although a cowboy at heart, Ted was eccentric and loved the glitzy life of Las Vegas – partying with celebrity guests, show-girls, strippers, and members of organized crime. He also had an affinity for drugs.

The Nevada Gaming Commission knew of Ted's drug use and association with organized crime, so they watched every move he made. When they asked Ted to submit to drug testing, he was livid. Knowing that drugs would stay in his hair much longer than in his bloodstream, Ted showed up for the drug test with his entire body shaved so they couldn't sample his hair.

Ted was inevitably arrested on drug trafficking charges. The conviction and his association with organized crime was too much for the Nevada Gaming Commission; in 1986 he was permanently banned from his management role at the Horseshoe.

Losing his role in the casino and the death of his father in 1989 weighed heavily on him. Having lost his livelihood, Ted relied more on drugs to occupy his time. He smoked marijuana and took Xanax, but his drug of choice was tar heroin. Ted, however, knew the dangers of drugs. His sister Barbara, who had similar drug problems, had committed suicide in 1977. Ted made a point to only smoke his heroin rather than inject it, reducing the chance that he could overdose.

Eventually Ted's wife took their daughter and left him. After she left, he spent more time in Las Vegas strip clubs where he met a young dancer named Sandy Murphy.

———

Sandy Murphy was a young, fit, strawberry-blonde beauty from Southern California. She had dropped out of high school and lived with an older man near the beach just south of Los Angeles, where she loved to surf. But in 1995, when that relationship fell apart, she and a girlfriend packed their bags and moved to Las Vegas.

At just twenty-one, Sandy arrived in Las Vegas with $15,000 and had never gambled in her life. By the end of the first night at Caesar's Palace, she had lost everything at the blackjack table.

Sandy's friend was a lingerie designer and the two girls started a business catering to Las Vegas strippers. The girls set up a table at a club called Cheetah's, where her friend sold the outfits and Sandy modeled them. When Ted saw Sandy modeling the Dallas Cowboys cheerleader outfit, he was hooked. That night he asked her to sit with him for a drink and they instantly hit it off.

Ted and Sandy started dating, but she didn't really know what he did for a living. Ted surely didn't look the part of a millionaire. He drove a pickup truck and wore cowboy boots and Levi's. So, when he took her to the Horseshoe and told her he owned it, she had her doubts. It didn't help his story when he explained that he couldn't go inside his own casino.

Although Sandy was less than half his age, she and Ted eventually fell in love and he moved her into his 8,500 square foot home. He bought her a convertible Mercedes and gave her a credit card with a $10,000 limit. She was thrust into a life of luxury.

Their relationship, however, didn't sit well with the rest of the Binion family. The family, particularly his eldest sister, considered Sandy a gold-digger who was only out for his money. His new relationship, coupled with his inability to be a part of the family business, drove a further wedge between Ted and his family.

Ted's excessive drug use fueled his paranoia. He didn't trust his family and he didn't trust banks. Since he could no longer enter the Horseshoe, he needed to move his belongings from a floor-to-ceiling vault that he kept in the casino's basement. The vault housed his massive silver collection that would need to be relocated.

On a small piece of land that he owned in the desert sixty miles west of Las Vegas, Ted had an underground concrete bunker built to house his valuables. The vault was built twelve feet below the surface of the desert floor. Inside he stored six tons of silver bullion, paper money, Horseshoe Casino chips, and over 100,000 rare coins, including extremely rare Carson City silver dollars. Those alone were believed to be worth as much as $14 million.

The construction of the bunker was extremely secretive. Only a few in Ted's immediate circle knew of its existence. He had commissioned a trucking company, MRT Transport, to build the huge bunker and secretly transport his collection from the Horseshoe to the new location. After the valuables were moved, only two people had the security code to enter the underground vault: Ted Binion and the owner of MRT Transport, Rick Tabish.

———

Ted had met Rick Tabish at a urinal, of all places. They struck up a conversation about Montana, where both men had spent time in their childhood. Although Tabish had previously been convicted of theft, he was a handsome smooth-talker and they developed a friendship. Rick quickly became an integral part of his life. Ted hired Rick to do odd jobs, which eventually led to the construction of the desert vault.

By mid-1998, Ted's drug use had escalated and his relationship with Sandy was going south. He became abusive and she was often seen with bruises – and, on one occasion, with a clump of hair missing. His paranoia was out of control; he took more drugs and carried a gun with him everywhere he went.

In early September, Ted got his next-door neighbor, a medical doctor, to write him a prescription for the anti-anxiety drug Xanax. The following day, Ted picked up the prescription himself at a nearby pharmacy. Then, on September 16, 1998, Ted bought twelve balloons of tar heroin from a dealer on the streets of Las Vegas.

Just before 4:00 p.m. the next day, Sandy Murphy walked into the home she shared with Ted Binion to find him lifeless on a yoga mat in the middle of the living room. An empty bottle of Xanax lay on the floor next to him. She frantically called 911, but he was gone. The medical examiner determined that Ted had overdosed on heroin and Xanax.

When police arrived, Sandy was crying over the death of Ted so hysterically that she had to be wheeled out of the house on a stretcher and taken to the hospital. Nurses at the hospital, however, noticed that her crying seemed overly theatrical. At times it seemed as if she were literally crying the words "boo hoo, boo hoo."

When she was allowed to go back into the house, she brought her attorney with her and videotaped the house. She believed that either the Binion family or the police had stolen many items from the house. Her intention in making the video was to take an inventory of the house, but this would later come back to bite her.

The news of Ted Binion's death was immediately on the television news. When Ted's lawyer heard the news, he contacted police. The lawyer said that Ted came to him just the day before his death and asked to have Sandy taken out of his will. The lawyer claimed that Ted no longer trusted her. Ted told him, "Take Sandy out of the will. If she doesn't kill me tonight. If I'm dead, you'll know what happened."

Las Vegas Police Sergeant Steve Huggins also had a strange conversation with Ted just before his death. Ted called the sergeant and told him that if he died, he should go to a small piece of land that he owned in Pahrump, Nevada. He told him that he had buried millions in silver and he wanted to make sure that it was given to his daughter.

———

Two days after Ted's death, police arrived at the desert vault at 2:00 a.m. to find Rick Tabish and two other men with a backhoe and a semi-trailer. They were digging up the vault. Tabish claimed that he was digging it up at Ted's instruction, to make sure that it got to his daughter Bonnie, but police didn't believe a word of his story. Tabish was arrested and charged with grand larceny. In an interesting twist, the following day Sandy

Murphy paid his bail. It became clear that Sandy and Tabish had been having an affair.

———

Five months had passed since Ted was buried with his cowboy boots and hat on top of his coffin. The Binion family didn't accept the coroner's report and pressed the police about Ted's official cause of death. They insisted that the medical examiner had made a mistake and Ted had not overdosed or committed suicide. They believed he was murdered by Sandy Murphy and Rick Tabish.

The Binion family had massive amounts of influence in Las Vegas and hired Tom Dillard, a former homicide detective turned private investigator, to look into Ted's death. In his opinion, everything pointed towards murder. With persuasion from the influential Binion family, the coroner reclassified Ted's death as a homicide. One month later, the Las Vegas police arrested Sandy Murphy and Rick Tabish and charged them with first degree murder, conspiracy, robbery, grand larceny, and burglary.

The Las Vegas district attorney hired a new medical examiner, Michael Baden. Baden was a celebrity among medical examiners, known for his high-profile work on the cases of OJ Simpson and Phil Spector. His more recent work included the autopsies of Jeffrey Epstein and George Floyd.

Baden disagreed with the original medical examiner's report. He believed that the red marks on Ted's chest were indentations from the buttons of his shirt. His theory showed the possibility that someone had sat upon his chest, depleting his air supply. He also pointed out that more red marks around Ted's mouth showed that he could have been smothered with a hand or a pillow. Baden hypothesized that he had been killed by a process called "burking."

Burking is when a victim is killed by someone sitting on the person's chest and simultaneously smothering them with a hand or pillow. This is usually while the victim is intoxicated. The process is known for leaving minimal evidence of a homicide.

Burking borrows its name from William Burke, who used the method to kill women in the late 1700s with his partner, William Hare. The duo sold the corpses for dissection at anatomy lectures.

At trial, the prosecution piled up the witnesses against both Sandy and Tabish. Baden presented his theory that Ted was killed by burking and claimed that almost no one dies from smoking heroin. The forensic pathologist testified that both heroin and Xanax were found in Ted's stomach, meaning that he had to have ingested the heroin rather than smoking it. It was an extremely unlikely way of consuming heroin which Ted had never done before.

A childhood friend of Rick Tabish testified that Tabish contacted him and asked him to help kill Ted. He claimed that Tabish offered him payment in silver and diamonds once the job was done. Another associate of Tabish claimed that he had bragged to him that he was Sandy Murphy's lover and was in the process of stealing Ted's buried treasure.

One of the most damning witnesses was Sandy's manicurist. She claimed that while getting her nails done three weeks prior to Ted's death, Sandy told her that Ted had a drug problem and he was going to overdose on heroin soon. She claimed that Sandy confided in her that after Ted's death, she would be rich and could be with her boyfriend.

The video that Sandy and her lawyer filmed of the house after Ted's death was brought into evidence by the prosecution. They claimed that the video showed Sandy taking a wine glass during the filming and placing it in her handbag. They hypothesized that the wine glass must have had evidence of a Xanax and heroin cocktail that she was hiding.

Murphy and her lawyer claimed the opposite - that the video showed proof that the house was not treated as a crime scene by the police and any evidence was either not preserved or had been contaminated.

There was no doubt that Ted Binion was a paranoid drug addict, but that didn't prove that he'd overdosed or committed suicide. After a two month trial and eight days of deliberation, both Tabish and Sandy were found guilty on twelve counts. At just twenty-eight years old, Sandy Murphy was sentenced to twenty-two years in prison; Tabish was sentenced to twenty-five. But that's not the end of the story.

———

Sandy didn't go to prison without a plan. Immediately after her sentencing, she wrote a thirty-page letter to Alan Dershowitz and asked if he would manage her appeal. Dershowitz was known for his work with the OJ Simpson case and got several letters every day from convicts around the country. However, Sandy's letter was convincing. After reviewing the evidence, he responded and took the case. He believed that Baden's evidence of burking was flawed.

All of Sandy's legal bills were paid for by a benefactor named Bill Fuller. The eighty-two-year-old was one of the most well-known music promoters in history. Throughout his career, he ran some of the most successful music venues in the world. He worked with a long list of musical acts including Johnny Cash, Patsy Cline, U2, Oasis, The Sex Pistols, and countless others. In the seventies, the eccentric Irishman moved to Nevada to prospect for gold. When he heard Sandy's story, he was intrigued. He said he was drawn to her because he believed in her innocence and her surname was Irish.

Sandy Murphy had spent four years in Florence McClure Women's Correctional Center, reminiscing her days surfing at Dana Point, when her conviction was overturned by the Nevada Supreme Court in July 2003.

Although both Sandy and Tabish had been convicted on twelve counts, the Judge had erred in deliberation. Tabish should have been tried separately for the assault and blackmail charge. Those charges were against another Las Vegas businessman and completely unrelated to the Ted Binion murder case. The judge also allowed testimony about Ted's will into evidence. The judge didn't inform the jury that the information was only a representation of Ted's state of mind—not as evidence that Sandy intended to kill him. Because of these errors, both Sandy and Tabish were granted a new trial.

At the second trial, Sandy didn't mess around. She and Tabish hired flamboyant civil rights attorney Tony Serra. Serra pointed out that the marks on Ted's chest could have been anything from dermatitis to skin cancer to even cigarette burns. Baden hadn't even examined Ted's body, only hypothesized based on photos from the original autopsy. To further disprove Baden's original testimony, the defense brought in nine medical experts who testified that his theory of burking was illogical.

During the second trial, Sandy's manicurist that had testified against her during the first trial admitted that the Binion family had paid her off. She received $20,000 from Ted's estate after her original testimony. Tabish's childhood friend whom testified in the first trial returned as well. This time, he claimed that Tabish was only kidding when he offered to pay him to kill Ted.

Their defense worked and both Sandy and Tabish were found not guilty of first degree murder charges. On the remaining cases of burglary and grand larceny, however, both were found guilty. Prosecutors hadn't claimed that she was with Tabish when he was digging up the silver, but charged her as a co-conspirator because she had paid Tabish's bail. Sandy was sentenced to time-served and was immediately released from jail.

Rick Tabish was also convicted of an additional charge of use of a deadly weapon and returned to prison. His original sentences were to run consecutively, but in 2009 his three convictions were reduced to run concurrently. In 2010, he was granted parole and released from prison.

Tabish moved to Butte, Montana, where he founded a startup providing services to the oil fracking industry. Years later, he founded and now manages a $100-million bitcoin mining operation. Besides a DUI conviction, Tabish has managed to stay out of trouble. In early 2020, however, his cryptocurrency business was temporarily shut down after a colleague of his was indicted for running a $722 million Ponzi scheme.

Sandy Murphy moved back to California, where she works as an artist and manages an art gallery with her husband in Laguna Beach. She has two children and goes by her married name, Sandy Pieropan.

CHAPTER 10
BLUE MIST #22

On a snowy January morning in 1972, eight-year-old Shelly Mickelson grabbed her coat and walked with a friend from her fourth-grade classroom at Marshall Elementary School toward her home in Flagstaff, Arizona. Like any other day, her mother expected her home for the lunch hour. But before Shelley made it past the baseball field between the school and her home, a familiar green Chevy Chevelle pulled up beside them. It was her neighbor, twenty-three-year-old Robert Moorman.

Moorman had received treatment for an intellectual disability and worked bussing tables at a nearby restaurant. He lived with his mother just a few blocks away from the Mickelson home and was known by Shelly's family. Earlier that week he had been to their home to ask what toys Shelly liked so he could buy something for her.

Moorman rolled down his passenger side window, called to Shelly, and told her that he was there to take her to lunch. "It's okay with your mom," he lied. Shelly had no reason to not trust him, got into his car, and the two drove off as the other girl continued her walk home.

It didn't take long for Shelly's mom to know something was wrong. As soon as she didn't show up for lunch, her mother called the school. One of the school officials had seen Shelly getting into the car, but thought nothing of it at the time, as Moorman was known by the school staff as well.

When she reported Shelly missing, a full-scale police manhunt was initiated and the media were immediately alerted. That evening, the story of the kidnapped girl was the lead story on the local television news channels.

Backtracking Moorman's movements, police learned that earlier that day he had asked for a $10 advance on his paycheck at the restaurant and cashed a $5 check at a local bank. He then borrowed a .22 pistol from a friend. At a local gun shop, he pawned two rifles for $60 and purchased ammunition for the handgun.

Late that evening, a motel manager in the tiny town of Ash Fork, Arizona, called the police. He had seen on the evening news that Moorman was wanted for kidnapping. The news piece showed photos of him, the young girl, and his green Chevy Chevelle. Although he hadn't seen Shelly, the motel manager recognized Moorman and the car. Moorman had checked into the motel using his real name and had told the manager that he was staying there with his niece.

Police instructed the motel manager to quickly move his own car behind Moorman's so he couldn't leave, but by the time he got off the phone, Moorman had disappeared with the girl. Moorman had seen the same nightly newscast. When police arrived and entered the motel room, all they found was the baseball hat he had been wearing earlier in the day, a section of rope, and pawn tickets for the two rifles.

Moorman had taken the girl to another motel near Kingman, Arizona. The next night they continued north to yet another motel in Lake Mead, on the border of Arizona and Nevada. Police and FBI meanwhile went from motel to motel throughout Northwest Arizona, but just missed him at every step.

The following morning Moorman was frustrated. He was running out of options and knew the police were onto him. It was only a matter of time before he would be apprehended. His frustration escalated when his Chevelle broke down on the side of the road. Furious, he got out and started walking away, leaving the young girl alone inside the car. January in northern Arizona was well below freezing. He knew Shelly would freeze to death in the abandoned car, but Moorman couldn't take Shelly's cries, eventually turning back and letting her out of the car.

He took her by the hand, put his thumb out, and walked with her down the side of the frozen highway. Although he felt sorry for the girl, he pitied himself more and wanted out of the stupid situation he had gotten himself into. If they didn't get someone to pick them up, Moorman's intention was to kill the girl and dump her body on the side of the road.

———

Mr. and Mrs. Swanson were traveling the country in their motor home when they saw Moorman and Shelly on the side of the road and offered them a ride. Shelly was cold and shivering – the couple could tell from her red eyes that she had been crying. Mrs. Swanson made them both some food in the back of the motor home as Mr. Swanson drove north toward Las Vegas. When Shelly had finished her food, Mrs. Swanson laid her on the bed in the back and told her to get some rest.

When she returned to the front of the motor home, Moorman had removed the bullets from his pistol, set it on the table, and asked if they had a drawer he could store his gun in. As they drove toward Las Vegas, the Swansons successfully persuaded him to surrender to the police. Moorman agreed and Mr. Swanson drove to the nearest police station.

———

Robert Moorman walked into the Las Vegas police station and placed his handgun and a pair of handcuffs on the desk in front of the desk sergeant. "I'm wanted for kidnapping a little girl," he said. The officer asked where the girl was and Moorman pointed below the edge of the officer's high desk. When the officer peered over his desk, he saw Shelly Mickelson.

Except for some light rope burns, Shelly seemed to be physically unharmed and the Mickelson family thought the horrible ordeal was over. When questioned by police, however, Shelly told them that she had been molested by Moorman. It was far from over for Robert Moorman, who faced kidnapping charges and was returned to Arizona.

———

Moorman had come to the attention of Flagstaff police in the past, but had never been arrested. Their first encounter with young Robert was when he accidentally shot and injured his mother. The second occasion was when he set their house on fire. Again, his mother covered for him and told police it was an accident. When he was sixteen, police were called to the Moorman house after he had used rope to tie up an eight-year-old girl. Claiming they were only playing "cowboys and Indians," Moorman was released without charges. His mother wasn't going to be able to get him out of the kidnapping charge, though.

During questioning after the kidnapping of Shelly, Moorman denied molesting the young girl, claiming he had blacked out and couldn't remember anything like that happening. He admitted that he intended to kill Shelly. He also initially intended to kill the Swansons, but when asked why he didn't, he replied, "Because they were nice to me."

Moorman's lawyer argued that he was mentally disabled and didn't understand the charges against him, but two psychiatrists provided by the prosecution disagreed. After examining him, both psychiatrists found that he was indeed mentally sound and able to stand trial.

> "His intelligence deficiency is so slight as to not be classified as mental retardation."

Both psychiatrists agreed that Moorman was neither a sociopath nor a psychopath; his only "illness" was a predilection for young girls. Although he had been prescribed medication to control his sexual appetite, Moorman had stopped taking it days before the kidnapping.

The judge agreed with the psychiatrists and concluded that Moorman was competent enough to stand trial and fully understood the charges against him.

In June 1972, Moorman pleaded guilty to the kidnapping charge. Before his sentencing, he gave a brief statement expressing his remorse and asked for another chance to begin a new life. But, despite his plea, Moorman was sentenced to nine years to life in prison.

———

Robert Moorman was born Robert "Bobby" Conger in 1948. His biological mother was just fifteen years old when she gave birth. She had been working as a prostitute, which left the identity of his father unclear. When his mother was seventeen, she broke her neck and died in a car crash. Two-year-old Robert was handed over to his grandparents, but life with them was no better. His grandfather was a violent, abusive alcoholic and Robert was inevitably sent to foster care.

Eventually he was adopted by the Moorman family just before his third birthday and renamed Robert Moorman. His adoptive father, Henry Moorman, was a successful businessman and ran a well-known taxi service in the Flagstaff area. By the time he was five years old, however, his adoptive father had passed away and Robert was left to be raised alone by his adoptive mother, Roberta "Maude" Moorman.

Growing up in Flagstaff, Moorman was a chubby boy who wore large, thick glasses and spoke in a childlike voice. Making friends was difficult and the other kids called him "slow" or "retarded." Relatives would later say that his mother was the only real friend that Robert ever had.

Maude Moorman insisted that Robert wasn't "retarded", but only a "slow learner in book matters." He had successfully completed high school and a course at a barber school. However, when he couldn't find work as a barber he enrolled in another course to become a hospital orderly. His mother claimed that before the kidnappings, Robert had never done anything violent in his life.

Maude supported her son and stayed by his side all throughout his life, including during his incarceration. For eleven years she took a bus more than 200 miles every month to visit her son in Florence, Arizona, a small town about an hour south of Phoenix that was home to the state prison.

In January 1979, after serving only seven years in prison, Moorman was paroled. However, his freedom didn't last long. He quickly returned to prison after he violated parole for possessing a weapon. Back in the Florence prison, Maude Moorman continued her routine of taking the bus regularly to visit her son.

Throughout the years Moorman continued to apply for parole, but was repeatedly denied. In lieu of parole, however, the prison had a program called "Compassionate Leave", in which well-behaved prisoners were granted temporary leave outside of the prison walls for short periods of time. Moorman had spent his time in prison being obedient and productive, so in 1983 was allowed compassionate leave three times. He used each opportunity to meet with his mother for 72 hours at a time.

On Thursday, January 12, 1984, Robert Moorman was granted compassionate leave a fourth time. He was allowed through the prison gate and walked to the Blue Mist Motel, just a quarter of a mile west of the prison. It was a small mid-century motel known for its bright blue paint. It resembled something straight out of an old movie, with the motel doors opening directly to the parked cars and a gated outdoor pool. As she had in the past, Maude Moorman was waiting for him in room 22.

————

Just before 7:00 a.m. the next morning, Moorman walked to a nearby convenience store where he purchased a folding buck knife, a steak knife, and some food. On his walk back to the motel, he stopped by a pizza parlor that was owned by a former prison guard that he knew. He told the owner that he was on furlough visiting his mother at the motel and they planned on coming back that evening for dinner, but she wasn't feeling well.

Blue Mist Motel and Robert Moorman

When Moorman returned to the Blue Mist Motel, he stopped by the office and spoke to the owner. He told Mr. Patel, who ran the motel with his wife, that his mother wasn't feeling well and there was no need to clean the room that day. As he left the office, he ran into Mrs. Patel who usually cleaned the rooms. Moorman told her that the room had a strange smell and asked to borrow some disinfectant spray. However as Mrs. Patel handed him the spray, she notice that it was Moorman that smelled putrid. He also seemed to have some spots on his face that looked like tiny drops of blood.

Later that morning, as Mrs. Patel cleaned the adjacent rooms, she noticed that Moorman had dropped several dirty towels outside the door. As she picked up the towels, she noticed they smelled worse than he did. The towels were ruined. There was no way that smell was coming out. Rather than wash them, Mrs. Patel threw them in the trash.

Later that afternoon, a friend of Maude's stopped by the hotel room looking for her. Marianne Southworth lived in Florence and visited with Moorman's mother every time she came down to see her son. When Robert answered the door, however, he claimed that his mother had gone to lunch and he wasn't sure where she was.

Marianne thought it was odd that Maude's purse was clearly visible on the table in the room. Even stranger was the temperature of the room. Despite the cold January afternoon, the air conditioner was running full-blast.

Later that afternoon, Moorman asked Mr. Patel if the dumpster behind the motel would be picked up in the morning. He explained that his mother had brought some meat with her from Flagstaff, but it had spoiled and he needed to get rid of it. Mr. Patel, however, explained that the garbage wasn't due to be picked up until the following Monday—three days later.

That evening, Moorman asked the owners of the pizza parlor and a nearby liquor store if he could use their dumpsters to get rid of "cow guts" that a friend had given him. It was an odd request to say the least and both business owners refused.

The pizza parlor owner had worked in the prison and was familiar with Moorman. He could tell that Robert looked nervous and worried. He knew something was wrong. On a hunch, he called the Florence police, who checked in on Moorman at 10:30 p.m. The officers knocked on room 22 of the Blue Mist Motel and told Moorman that they had heard that his mother was not feeling well and they were there to check in on her.

Wearing only a pair of unzipped pants and a belt, Moorman explained that his mother had left around 6:00 p.m. that evening with a Mexican woman and he didn't know where she was, telling them, "I'm getting worried about her because she didn't take her medication with her."

When the officers asked why he was trying to get rid of "cow guts," he replied, "A friend gave them to me. But I got rid of them.

I just flushed them down the toilet." Before the officers left the motel, they peeked into the dumpster behind the motel to make sure Moorman wasn't lying. Nothing seemed out of the ordinary, but they felt he was hiding something. The officers then drove to the prison to ask the guards for a description of Mrs. Moorman.

Late that night, Moorman was troubled. He really needed to get rid of that "meat." Moorman called the prison and spoke to a guard he knew, claiming he had twenty-five pounds of dog bones that he thought the prison dogs would like. The prison guard thought it was strange, but agreed to help him. He showed up at the motel a few minutes later with his truck, took the box of bones, and drove back to the prison.

Not long after the guard arrived back at the prison, he received a phone call from the officers that had spoken to Moorman earlier that evening. When they mentioned that Moorman's mother was missing and Moorman had been acting suspiciously, the guard told them about the box of bones he had just picked up.

When the officers arrived at the prison and opened up the box, they found trash bags filled with bones, but the officers thought they were too big to be dog bones. They believed they were human. The officers took the box and drove to the hospital - medical staff would know for sure.

While they waited for results, the officers drove back to the motel and found Moorman using the payphone near the office. As he walked from the payphone back to his room, they told him they would wait there with him until his mother arrived home and suggested that he wait with them in the squad car.

The three of them sat in the car for over an hour until two officers from the prison arrived and parked next to them. The results had come back from the hospital and the bones were indeed human.

Moorman was handcuffed and said to the officers,

"I wonder if I need a lawyer. I'll leave it up you guys whether I need a lawyer."

When police entered room 22 at the Blue Mist Motel, the bath towels, bedding, bathroom walls, tub, and bathroom floor were all covered in blood. A buck knife, a steak knife, and a scouring sponge still had human tissue on them. Strangely, his mother's bra hung in the closet with $500 in cash pinned to it.

Although there was no question he had butchered his mother in the room, there was no sign of her body. It didn't take long, however, to find her remains. In a dumpster behind the motel police found Maude's head, torso cut in two pieces, feet, and hands. Each were wrapped in plastic bags. The hands were missing their fingers. They also found the packaging for the knives, a pair of his mother's pajamas, and a razor. Another bag was filled with random bits of muscle, skin, and tissue. Only one finger was recovered from the sewer.

In Moorman's personal belongings in his prison cell, they found a notebook with odd writings such as instructions on how to train a dog to make deposits at a bank. However, investigators were most concerned with a document entitled "last will and testament."

Maude Moorman had already written a will that left everything to her son, but her assets totaling approximately $200,000 were to be put into a trust in his name. He would only have access to the interest it created. She didn't believe he was mentally or fiscally able to handle that much money all at once.

Robert didn't like that idea and had drawn up an amendment to the will. His amendment would have put the assets into a company called RHM Enterprises. RHM Enterprises, however, didn't actually exist and his mother hadn't signed the will. The amendment was dated January 13, the day he murdered her.

When Moorman arrived at the police station, he told detectives, "You can change the charge. She's dead." He told police that he "lost his cool" when his mother asked him to "take my father's place and do things I couldn't handle." He claimed that his mother had forced him to have sex with her ever since he was a child.

> "My mom and I had a… we had an argument, and during it I hit her a few times, and then it got worse and I… I lost my cool and I tied her up, and she kept on me, talkin' about things that, um… pertained to my real family and, I don't remember the exact time, and I suffocated her."

He explained that they were having sex and he put a pillow over her face to suffocate her.

> "Then I took the 409 (cleaning spray) and went into the wash room. I panicked, at which time I dissected her."

A postmortem examination of what was left of Maude's body, however, showed no sign of sexual activity. No semen was found on the sheets or clothes. The medical examiner noted that the dismemberment was meticulous. He had cut her feet at the ankles, hands at the wrists, and fingers at the knuckles.

Moorman told police that he had flushed nine of her fingers down the toilet. One finger had rolled away as he cut it off, and he lost it. He later flushed that one too, which was found in the sewer.

At trial, his lawyers again claimed that Moorman didn't know what he was doing and was mentally unable to understand the severity of his crimes. They argued that he had endured years of abuse from his adoptive mother, forcing him to perform sex acts on her which provoked his actions, but family members disputed his claim. By all accounts, his mother was loving and the best friend he ever had.

The jury agreed and found that he was sane. The way he dismembered the body showed that he knew the difference between right and wrong. Moorman was convicted of first-degree murder and was sentenced to death on May 7, 1985.

For thirty-seven years Moorman sat on death row awaiting execution, during which time his health deteriorated considerably. In the years leading up to his execution, Moorman suffered a stroke and received both an appendectomy and a quadruple bypass. Despite several appeals, he was finally scheduled for lethal injection with only two days' notice.

On February 29, 2012, Robert Moorman requested a double hamburger, French fries, two beef burritos, two 14 ounce containers of rocky road ice cream, and three RC Colas before his dose of pentobarbital. Because one of the drugs used for execution at the time had expired, his execution used only a single drug, rather than the standard three-drug cocktail.

His last words were an apology directed at the family of Shelly Mickelson, "I hope this brings closure and they can start healing now. I just hope they will forgive me in time."

CHAPTER 11
THE CRYBABY KILLER

Tami Engstrom had spent her entire life in the area around Youngstown, Ohio, midway between Cleveland and Pittsburgh. On a cold February evening in 1991, twenty-two-year-old Tami dropped her eighteen-month-old son off with her best friend, Sharon King, and drove to work.

Tami worked as a bartender at the Clover Bar in Hubbard, Ohio. Her shift started at 6:30 p.m., but she wasn't feeling well and called her mother at 9:00 p.m. and asked her to cover for her. Her mother, Elizabeth Heiss, worked at the same bar and came to cover the rest of her shift at 9:30 p.m.

When Tami left the Clover, however, she wasn't quite ill enough to go directly home just yet. Her friend was already watching her baby and there was a drinking event scheduled that evening at the Nickelodeon Lounge where her uncle, Daniel Hivner, was a regular patron. The Nickelodeon was another in a long list of dive bars in the area. It sat in Brookfield Township in the tiny town of Masury, Ohio, just a few hundred feet away from Ohio's border with Pennsylvania.

The Nickelodeon Bar and Tami Engstrom

Tami had several drinks with her uncle and showed off her new diamond ring she had purchased a few weeks before. It was a large ring with a cluster of diamonds that she had bought from her friend, Sharon, for $1,200.

Tami drank throughout the night with her uncle, a few other friends at the bar, and a man she met that night; thirty-two-year-old Kenneth Biros. Biros was a friend of her uncle. Although Tami didn't know him, Biros was well known in the bar and throughout the Youngstown area. He grew up and graduated high school in Youngstown before attending Youngstown State University as a geology major. Although it took him thirteen years, he finally got a degree. He had worked on an Alaskan fishing boat for a brief time, but most recently worked laying asphalt.

Despite feeling ill, Tami continued drinking. As midnight rolled around, she set her head on the bar table and, before long, she had completely passed out. When she fell off of her seat and onto the floor, Daniel helped her back into a booth and let her sleep for a bit. The bar was preparing to close at 1:00 p.m. and Daniel woke Tami and helped her out to the parking lot. He told her he would drive her home, but when he took her keys she became upset. She insisted she was fine to drive home, but she clearly wasn't.

That's when Kenneth Biros offered to take Tami to an all-night diner to get her some coffee with hopes that it would sober her up. He would then bring her back to the Nickelodeon Lounge and Daniel could decide if she could drive home herself. At 1:15 a.m., Tami and Biros left the bar in Biro's car as Daniel stayed after-hours with friends at the Nickelodeon.

———

That same evening, Tami's husband, Andy, had gone to the Clover Bar to see her. When Tami's mother told him that she went home sick, he drove to their house, but she wasn't there. He called her sister, who told him that she probably went to the Nickelodeon. Just after 1:00 a.m. Andy called the Nickelodeon and was mistakenly told that Tami and her uncle Daniel had left the bar and were on their way home. Andy wasn't worried and went to bed that night assuming she would walk in at any minute.

Daniel waited at the Nickelodeon, expecting Tami and Biros to return, but neither of them showed.

The next morning, Andy woke in a shock when he found that Tami never came home. He drove to the Nickelodeon to find Tami's car still sitting in the parking lot. Daniel informed him that Kenneth Biros had given her a ride the night before.

Andy showed up at Biros' home to ask where Tami was. Biros said that after they left the bar, he only drove about three blocks before,

"I tapped her on the shoulder and she freaked out. She got out of the car and started running through people's yards on Davis Street."

Andy told him he was going to file a police report and,

"If she don't turn up right fast, they are gonna come looking for you, and it's gonna be your ass!"

The area where Biros claimed that Tami had jumped out of the car was across the state line in Sharon, Pennsylvania. That day, Andy filed a missing person's report.

Biros was confronted by several members of Tami's family and friends. Each time he gave a similar explanation: she had jumped out of the car and he hadn't seen her since. He claimed that he chased her between houses for a while, but she was too fast and he didn't want to raise attention because he had been driving after having several drinks.

Tami's uncle, however, noticed that Biros had a scratch above his right eye that wasn't there the night before. There were also scratches on his hands that he didn't notice the night before at the Nickelodeon.

Biros claimed that he scratched his hand when he got home that night. He had locked himself out of the house and had to break a window. The scratch above his eye, he claimed, was from chopping wood early the next morning.

Both Tami's brother Tom and her father James didn't believe Biro's story. "If you put one scratch on my daughter, I'll kill you!" screamed her father. Tom told Biros, "I'll rip your heart out."

Biros reassured James,

"Don't worry. Your daughter is going to be just fine. You wait and see."

———

That evening, Biros helped friends and family search the area where he claimed Tami jumped out of the car. After hours of searching, they found nothing.

When Biros returned home where he lived with his mother and brother, his mother had found a gold ring on the bathroom floor and asked him about it. "I have no idea. It looks like cheap gold," he told her. His mother disagreed. It was not a cheap ring. He told his mother that it could have belonged to the girl that jumped out of his car the night before. He took the ring and told his mother he would take it back to the Nickelodeon, but instead he hid it.

As Tami's friends and family continued the search, police called Biros and instructed him to come to the police station to give his statement. Except for an arrest for driving under the influence of alcohol, Biros had no prior police record. Police from both Brookfield Township, Ohio, and Sharon, Pennsylvania, were present at the interview since the disappearance happened literally on the state line.

During the interview, Biros gave a near identical story that he had told Tami's family, but this time he gave more detail. He claimed that Tami had passed out in the car. He stopped at a bank teller machine to get some cash and, when he returned to the car, she woke up and screamed at him. She wanted him to drive her back to the Nickelodeon. When he told her they were on their way to get some coffee, she jumped out of the car and ran.

The police Captain John Klaric from Sharon, Pennsylvania, had some doubts about his story. As the interview pressed on, Captain Klaric asked him if he had made sexual advances toward Tami. Biros had told Tami's husband that he only tapped her on the shoulder, but he told Tami's uncle that he accidentally touched her knee. Klaric knew there was more to this story.

Captain Klaric gave Biros his theories. He suggested maybe he made a sexual advance, she denied him, and then she ran out of the car. Initially Biros denied the idea, but when Klaric added that maybe Tami "accidentally" hit her head, Biros stopped him. Biros asked to speak to Klaric alone, then the other officers left the room.

Biros then told Klaric that his hypothesis was exactly what had happened. He added,

"And I've done something very bad."

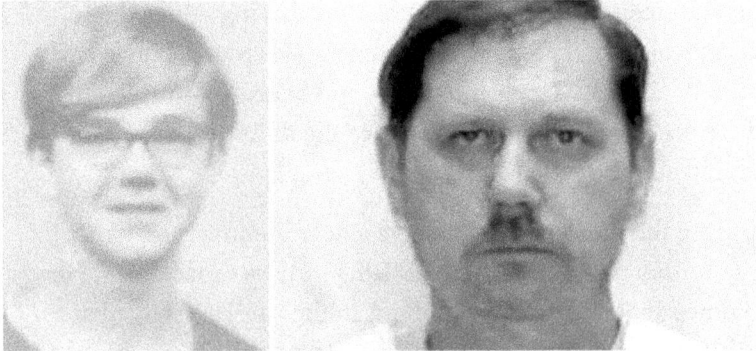

Kenneth Biros (high school & mugshot)

"It's like you said. We were in the car together. We were out along the railroad tracks. I touched her on the hand. Then I went further. I either touched or felt her leg, but she pushed my hand away. The car wasn't quite stopped. She opened the door and fell and struck her head on the tracks."

Biros went on to explain that Tami had died next to the railroad tracks near his home on King Graves Road in Brookfield Township.

Biros was immediately arrested and he repeated the story for the other officers—Tami had hit her head and died along the railroad tracks. But when they asked where her body was, he asked for an attorney. After speaking to his attorney, he agreed to take police to the body, but they weren't quite ready for what they would find.

———

On Sunday, February 10, Biros took police forty miles east to Butler County, Pennsylvania. There they found parts of Tami's body. He then drove them thirty miles north to Venango County, Pennsylvania, where they found more body parts.

Biros had been busy that night. He had severed her head and right breast from the torso, while her right leg had been cut off above the knee. Her black leg stockings had been pushed to her ankles. Tami's torso had been butchered. Biros had cut her open and removed her organs. Her anus, rectum, and most of her genitalia had been removed and were never found.

After a search of the area next to the railroad tracks, detectives found massive amounts of blood on the gravel. In a nearby swamp they found pieces of her intestines, gallbladder, liver, and bowels. Later searches of the area uncovered her black leather coat with knife marks near the collar. Tami's black shoes were found with a single pubic hair inside that matched her DNA.

A search of Biros' home provided a pocket knife covered in dried blood. The long brown coat and tennis shoes that Biros had worn to the bar that evening were in his bedroom, also covered with blood. Tami's blood and pieces of her liver were found in the trunk of his car.

Despite the extensive butchering, sexual mutilation, and dismemberment of Tami's body, an autopsy revealed she died of strangulation. Biros had strangled her with his bare hands for almost five minutes before she finally died. The medical examiner counted ninety-one stab wounds, all of which were inflicted after she was already dead. There were also five blunt force wounds on the top of her head from the knife handle, or possibly his fist.

Kenneth Biros was charged with aggravated murder, attempted rape, aggravated robbery, and felonious sexual penetration. If found guilty, he faced a death sentence.

———

During his trial, Biros' defense told of how he grew up with a verbally and emotionally abusive father that denied him affection and constantly berated the entire family. They explained that until the murder, Biros had been a normal member of society with very little trouble with the law.

Biros testified on his own behalf and provided yet another scenario of what had happened that night. Throughout his testimony he wept profusely, garnering the nickname "The Crybaby Killer" from the press. During his testimony he claimed that, when he returned from the bank teller machine, he reached over and shook Tami, who had passed out in his car. When she woke up, she was too drunk to tell him where she lived, so he took her home to allow her to "sleep it off."

He explained that he parked within a few hundred feet of his home and tried to wake her again. When she awoke this time, she screamed at him,

"I don't know you! Where are we?"

He went on to claim that she started hitting him and he hit her with his forearm. That was when she opened the door and started running along the railroad tracks. He explained that he tried to catch up to her with his car and inadvertently hit her. When she fell, her head hit the gravel.

Biros claimed he rolled Tami onto her back and saw that her head was bleeding. She had hit her head against the railroad track. He told the court that Tami screamed and threw rocks at him and he pulled out his pocket knife to "calm her down." Tami, however, was able to take the knife away from him, which scratched his hands. He then pinned her down and placed his hands over her mouth. He didn't realize until after he removed his hands that he had smothered her.

After realizing what he had done, he panicked, went home, and cleaned himself up. Twenty minutes later, he returned to the body. He was angry at himself and angry at Tami, believing that she had destroyed his life. He told the court that he then removed Tami's clothes because they were "in the way" and started stabbing.

He then dragged the body into the woods. As he grabbed her hands, he noticed her gold ring. He claimed he took off the ring and put it in his pocket to keep it from digging into his hands as he dragged her. When he tried to bury her, he realized that her body was too big for the hole he had dug. Rather than making the hole bigger, he cut off her head and leg. He then buried those parts in another location and buried her clothes separately from the body parts.

The next day, as Biros washed his car, he realized that Tami's purse was still in the car. He took it into his house and burned it in the fireplace. The following evening, after Tami's friends and family members threatened him, he got worried that the body would be found so close to his house. He dug up the body parts and buried them in two separate locations across the state line in Pennsylvania.

During his testimony, Biros denied that he had told police that he made any sexual advances toward Tami and had no excuse for removing her sexual organs, anus, and rectum. He told the court he had no recollection of where those parts were. He also denied hitting Tami on the top of her head with the knife handle or his fists.

———

The autopsy and testimony of a forensic pathologist, however, poked holes in Biros' new story. He claimed to have stabbed her using only a pocket knife, but evidence proved that a much larger knife was used. The incisions around the genitals were inflicted with much more precision than a pocket knife would have provided. Additionally, there was no evidence that the victim had been struck by a car. Finally, the autopsy showed that her hyoid bone had been fractured and there was damage to the tissue around her neck. This could only have happened by strangulation, not by suffocation, as Biros claimed.

It didn't matter what story he gave; he was going down one way or the other. Biros was found guilty on all counts, sentenced to death, and scheduled for execution by lethal injection.

A year before his scheduled execution, Tami's sister, Debi Heiss, urged the Attorney General to deny Biros' pleas for leniency:

"Kenneth Biros beat, tortured, sexually assaulted, mutilated, dismembered, and robbed Tami with no remorse. He has been given more humanity and mercy from the state than my sister ever had. It's time for justice to be served. Tami was my sister and my best friend. She was raped, she was tortured for hours. She had to be so scared that night."

Biros was eventually executed on December 8, 2009. He was added to the Guinness Book of World Records for being the first person in the United States to be put to death using a single-drug large dose of sodium thiopental, an anesthetic.

Twenty years after her death, Tami's friend Sharon King wrote about her theories that the murder was part of a still-continuing satanic cult in the area. She claimed that when Tami left the bar that night, her fingernails were painted red. However, when her body was recovered her nails had been painted black. She also claimed that Tami's corpse had been branded with the numbers 666, while her veins were completely dry when her body was found. Police records, however, mention none of those claims.

Additional unsubstantiated stories on the Internet claim that Biros had taken Tami to a shed behind his house where he butchered her. Because of these stories, some people believe the Biros' house – which has since burned down – is still haunted by the ghost of Tami Engstrom.

CHAPTER 12
THE DARLINGTON CANNIBAL

Julie Paterson had never really had it easy living in Darlington, in the northeast of England. When she was just an infant, her mother died of a brain tumor, leaving her and her three-year-old brother, Michael, to be raised by their father.

By the time she was thirty-two years old, she had four children but had lost custody of three of them. She shared the youngest child with her boyfriend, Alan Taylor. Throughout her life Julie had been prone to depression, which was amplified by her addiction to alcohol and Valium.

Julie Paterson and Alan Taylor

Alan knew Julie well and was used to her bouts of depression. He also knew that it wasn't unusual for her to go to a pub in Darlington and not return for a few days. She had been gone as long as a week in the past, but never longer.

In April 1998, Julie left for a pub and didn't come home the next day. As the days went by, Alan initially didn't worry. It wasn't the first time. However, when Julie missed an appointment to visit her eldest daughter, he knew something was wrong. That was one appointment that Julie would never miss.

He searched their local neighborhood, checked the local pubs, and called her friends and family. When nobody had heard from her, he called Darlington police to report her missing.

Since she had already been missing several days, police immediately started searching local parks, woodlands, rivers, and ponds. After days of searching, there was still no sign of Julie.

On May 16, 1998, a police dog picked up the scent of a human near a fence along a rarely travelled footpath. On the other side of a fence was a dilapidated house with an overgrown garden. The dog handler assumed the property was abandoned and entered the garden. The property wasn't abandoned, however, and a woman came out of the door to ask what he was doing. When he explained that his dog had picked up on a scent, the woman pointed toward the edge of the garden and explained that there was a garbage bag beneath a shrub. She said some boys had thrown it over the fence several days before. She told the officer she assumed it contained a dead dog because it had started to smell. As soon as the officer opened the bag, he knew it was the smell of decomposition. But it wasn't a dog. It was human.

A forensic examination determined it was Julie Paterson, but it wasn't all of her. The bag contained only a torso. Both legs, both arms, and the head were missing.

Before the news of Julie's death had hit the newspapers, a man named David Harker was in a local pub bragging to friends that he had "killed a girl called Julie." Twenty-four-year-old Harker, however, was a man known for telling tall tales and none of his friends took him seriously.

Harker had lived his entire life in the northeast of England and had trouble with the law at an early age. As a boy, he tortured and mutilated small animals. At just sixteen, he attacked two men and their dog, resulting in the death of the dog. For this attack, he was sent to a young offender's institution for a brief time.

But there were two sides to Harker. To most of his friends and acquaintances, he seemed like a good kid. He was charming, popular, and outgoing. His good looks made him a hit with the ladies, so he had no problem finding women to have sex with him.

In his later teen years, Harker sang for a punk band called Downfall and many young kids in the punk-rock scene admired and looked up to him. On the sides of his shaved head he had tattooed the names of his favorite punk bands: Disorder and Subhumans.

Harker spoke up against racists and sex offenders; he came across as polite and respectful. But when his girlfriend and the mother of his four-year-old son left him, he fell into a deep depression. His drinking increased and he became belligerent and angry. His anger issues got him banned from many pubs in the town. On one occasion, he got so angry that he put his fist through a pub window.

Harker was also an avid fan of true crime, reading every book about serial killers he could find. He often told his friends he would be a great serial killer because he knew so much about how to not get caught. His nickname for himself was "Devil Man."

———

Harker had bragged to no less than twenty-eight friends that he had killed a girl named Julie. Because he was usually drunk when he made the claim, none of his friends believed him. However, when the discovery of Julie's torso reached the newspapers, his friends reconsidered the possibility.

The evening after the news was released, several of his best friends speculated possibilities. Together, they read the article in the newspaper over and over. Could he have been telling the truth? Was he really capable of that level of mayhem? That night, Harker's best friend walked into a Darlington police station and told them of Harker's boasts.

Just days before his friends went to police, Harker had been arrested on a robbery charge and was awaiting trial at a bail hostel. With Harker already in custody, detectives obtained a warrant and searched his apartment. It was immediately obvious that his friends were correct; Harker was the killer.

The apartment walls and floor were literally covered in dark red, dried blood. It was clear that he had killed her in the apartment. He made no attempt to clean the crime scene. Bloody drag marks led from the hallway near the stairs to the kitchen. The kitchen had several large hooks attached to the ceiling and the whole place smelled dank and musky. The basement of his apartment was even bloodier than the main level. A forensic team matched the blood in his apartment to Julie Paterson and clothes found in the basement belonged to Julie.

The apartment itself was stark, yet messy. On the walls he had scribbled macabre lyrics to his favorite heavy metal songs. The floor could barely be seen through a layer of garbage and beer cans. His bedroom contained only an old mattress on the floor surrounded by various porn magazines. On his bookshelf police found several books about serial killers, a book about how to survive in prison, and another on how to dodge questions during a police interview.

———

Police arrested Harker at the bail hostel where he was being held. During questioning, he initially denied killing Julie despite the overwhelming evidence at his apartment and the statements of several close friends. Eventually, however, he confessed and told detectives the gruesome details of the murder.

———

Harker and Julie met one evening in April at a pub in Darlington. After a night of drinking, Harker charmed his way into getting her back to his apartment. Once there, they had consensual sex – but in the middle of intercourse, he claimed that he "got bored" and strangled her with one of her own stockings.

David Harker and his Darlington apartment

As her body lay there on the mattress, he had sex with her cold corpse. The next day, he cut a chunk of flesh from her thigh using a kitchen knife, placed it in a pan, cooked it with garlic, pasta, and cheese, and ate it. Harker then dragged her to the basement, where he wiped the body with bleach and kept her for several weeks. Using a saw, he cut off her head, arms, and legs. Detectives knew what he did with the torso, but Harker refused to say what he did with the head, arms, and legs.

During interviews with psychiatrists, Harker said,

"People like me don't come from those films. Those films come from people like me."

He told them that his ambition was to become Britain's youngest and most notorious serial killer. He was destined to get caught, however, because he couldn't help but boast about his crime.

———

David Harker pleaded guilty to manslaughter on grounds of diminished responsibility. The sentence was essentially the same as a murder charge—life imprisonment with eligibility for parole in fourteen years. At his sentencing, one of the psychiatrists that analyzed Harker said that he was pure evil; that no hospital treatment could be given for him. He suffered from multiple mental disorders and putting him in a mental institution would be a waste of time. The psychiatrist determined that he was in the top four percent of Britain's most disturbed men. As a result, he was sent to a high security prison rather than a mental hospital.

At sentencing, the judge told Harker,

"You are an evil and exceptionally dangerous man. You killed her in the most terrible circumstances and dismembered her body. You glorified in her death and the manner of her death. I have no doubt that given the slightest opportunity you will kill again."

———

Even in prison, Harker basked in his depravity. Despite Julie's family's requests, he refused to tell what he had done with the rest of her body. Freddie Newman, the father of two of Julie's children, sent letters to Harker in prison, but he only replied with words of torment:

"It's always good to know that people are thinking of me, especially those who suffer because of my actions.

You are correct when you speak of decency, I have none. I have no inhibitions, remorse or regret, and therefore care not one bit if your wife has a full body burial or not.

I hope you are happy in the knowledge that you don't suffer alone in your loss. Your wife was not the first or the last person I killed.

You ask why I have done this evil thing. Well, I could intellectualise endlessly about murder, mutilation, decapitation and cannibalism but a man of your intellect wouldn't be able to grasp any of it.

So to give you something you could understand, I killed all the people I did because I enjoyed it.

Do you hate the evil man who chopped up and ate your wife? I am not evil Mr Newman but I am a monster.

Don't bother writing to me again or I will show you terror unbound. I do have your address now.

Goodbye Mr Newman."

Freddie Newman never recovered from Julie's death and eventually committed suicide in 2006.

———

Alan Taylor, the father of Julie's youngest child and her partner at the time of her death, suffered from the loss as well. It consumed him. Taylor became obsessed with trying to find the missing parts of Julie and spent years digging holes in the ground all over Darlington.

He would often weep over her gravesite and say,

"How can she be at rest? She's not even here."

Like Freddie Newman, Alan Taylor also took an extreme measure. In 2006 he had given up all hope of finding Julie's remains and, in an alcoholic rage, strangled his best friend, John Morrison, with a belt.

When asked his motivation for killing his best friend, he told police that he wanted to commit a crime of the same level as Harker. He claimed that his alcoholism and post-traumatic stress disorder (PTSD) since Julie's death had left him a broken man. He felt that his only option was to be sent to the same prison as Harker so he could get his revenge.

At his sentencing, however, the judge realized that he wanted revenge and sent him to a different prison to Harker. Taylor was sentenced to life in prison and his hopes of ever finding the remains of Julie Paterson were gone. Three months into his prison sentence, he committed suicide in his cell.

Nine years after the murder, the Darlington Police Chief Superintendent who worked the case made one last-ditch effort before his retirement. He visited Harker's prison with hopes of getting him to talk, but Harker refused to see him. He told prison guards,

"If anyone from the Durham Constabulary comes to see me, I will tell them to piss off."

More than twenty years after her murder, Julie's family still struggles with the loss.

CHAPTER 13
BONUS CHAPTER: THE HOMESCHOOLERS

This chapter is a **free bonus chapter** from True Crime Case Histories: Volume 5

———

It's not clear what life was like for Hana Alemu in Ethiopia, but it's hard to imagine it could have been worse than it became when the eleven-year-old was adopted by the Williams family in Sedro-Woolley, Washington.

———

Larry and Carri already had seven children of their own and wanted more, but her last pregnancy had left Carri Williams unable to bear more children. It had become a trend for home-schooling evangelical Christians in the mid-2000s to adopt needy children into their already large families. The families felt that it was a duty of their faith to rescue children that needed a good home and then homeschool them according to a conservative Christian curriculum. Other families from their Bible study group had adopted as many as eight children into their lives; Carri and Larry wanted the same.

Larry Williams worked from noon until midnight as a millwright for Boeing, while Carri stayed home to homeschool their kids. Carri had attended a women's retreat run by a ministry called Above Rubies. During the retreat, they spoke of the trend among evangelicals to adopt children from Liberia, a west African country experiencing political instability caused by multiple civil wars.

In 2008, the Williamses contacted Adoption Advocates International (AAI), a secular adoption agency based in Port Angeles, Washington. AAI was run by a woman named Merrily Ripley who had twenty children; three biological and seventeen adopted. Merrily informed Carri that there were two orphaned children in Ethiopia that needed a loving home. One child was deaf and Carri had studied American Sign Language before getting married, so it seemed like a perfect match.

To prepare for the adoption, the Williamses took a quick home-study course provided by AAI and filled out the necessary paperwork. AAI apparently missed the fact that Carri had left one section of the paperwork blank: the part about their beliefs on child discipline.

In the months leading up to the adoption, Carri and Larry saw a one-minute video clip of the children crying and begging for a good home. It was heart wrenching. Seven-year-old Immanuel was deaf and eleven-year-old Hana was slightly underweight at only 77 pounds.

Immanuel and Hana had been living in the Kidane Mehret orphanage in the Ethiopian capital city of Addis Abada. Both had been abandoned at an early age. Though they were not related, they were excited that they would soon become brother and sister living in the United States. Learning that their new parents lived in the idyllic countryside of the Pacific Northwest, Hana naively read *Little House on the Prairie* in preparation for her new, exciting life.

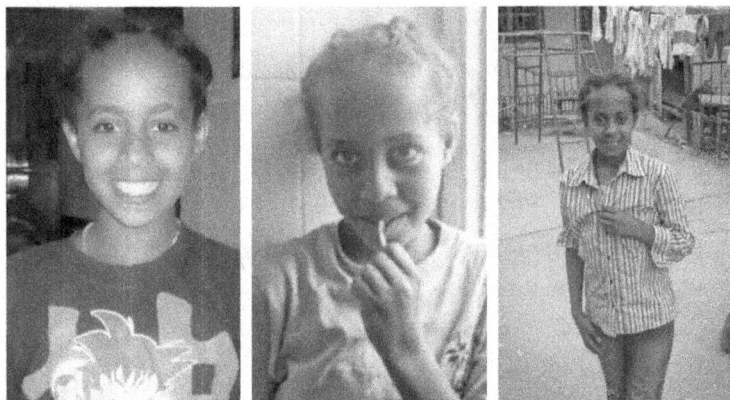

Hana Williams (Right photo in Ethiopia)

In the months after Hana and Immanuel's arrival in 2008, the Williams' post-adoption reports came to AAI as per the adoption agreement. According to the adoption agency, everything in the reports seemed normal and Hana had filled out to a healthier 105 pounds. However, in June 2009, the reports suddenly stopped. Although the adoption agreement stated that Carri and Larry would continue to send reports throughout the children's lives, technically they were under no legal obligation to file the reports. The adoption agency had no way of knowing the atrocities that were going on in the Williams household.

Larry and Carri Williams believed in a strict fundamentalist Christian lifestyle. In addition to homeschooling their children, almost all television and Internet access was prohibited. They believed women should never wear pants, only skirts or dresses and never swimsuits, and certainly never vote. The children were rarely seen in a public setting and only socialized with a select few like-minded families. Larry regularly preached to the children in the backyard of their rural five-acre property.

As for disciplining the children, the Williamses adhered to the teachings of a controversial book called *To Train Up A Child* by Michael and Debi Pearl. The book taught that the principles and techniques for training an animal and raising a child were the same. It instructed parents to begin spanking their children within the first few months of birth to "break their will."

In his book, Michael Pearl's argument for beating a child came straight from his interpretation of the Bible. Pearl believed that Proverbs 13:24 justified his beliefs:

"He that spareth his rod hateth his son."

Pearl said,

"A child properly and timely spanked is healed in the soul and restored to wholeness of spirit. A child can be turned back from the road to hell through proper spankings."

The book went into great detail of specific implements for parents to use; a wooden spoon, spatula, or the most popular weapon — a short length of small plastic plumbing tubing. This was a particularly well-liked implement because it could be easily curled up and kept available in a parent's pocket at all times. The book also taught parents to withhold food and put children under a cold outdoor garden hose as punishment.

The Pearls' book was extremely popular with fundamentalist Christian homeschoolers and, according to the author, sold almost 700,000 copies in the first seven years of its publication. The Pearls' No Greater Joy ministry generated upwards of $1.7 million tax-free dollars per year.

––––––––

For the next two years, Hana's hopes of the American dream quickly washed away. Life with the Williams family was nothing like the *Little House on the Prairie* life she had envisioned.

Within months after Hana arrived in the United States, she began menstruating. This infuriated Carri, who told members of her knitting group that she had wanted to adopt "a little girl, not a half-grown woman." She complained that Hana was rebellious, telling her knitting friends, "I wouldn't wish her on anyone."

Friends and neighbors of the Williams family had noticed that Hana and Immanuel were often absent from public family outings, holidays, trips to town, or to church. On the rare occasion that they were brought to church with the family, one parishioner that knew sign language often attempted to sign with Immanuel, but Carri and Larry didn't want him communicating with anyone. One of them would quickly whisk the boy away before he had a chance to converse.

Neighbors noticed the seven children would be seen actively playing together at the front of the Williams' home, while Hana and Immanuel would be left standing alone near the driveway staring at their feet.

At home, the discipline was much worse than anyone could have imagined. Hana had Hepatitis B, which again infuriated Carri, who accused her of purposely smearing blood on the bathroom walls. Because of this, Hana was not allowed to use the bathroom in the house. She was only allowed to use a filthy outdoor portable toilet behind the barn that was only serviced twice a year.

The indoor shower was off limits too. Regardless of temperature, Hana's shower was a garden hose propped up with sticks in the front yard. Hana was often forced to use the cold makeshift shower while the other children watched from the windows of the warm house.

When Hana made any sort of complaint about the clothes that Carri had chosen for her to wear, she would lose her right to wear clothes at all, and given only a towel to wear for the day.

Hana had long braided hair that she was proud of. Her hair was the one thing she could take pride in and Carri knew it. The first spring of Hana's new life, she was told to cut the grass in the yard. When she finished, the grass was cut shorter than Carri had wanted it. As punishment, Carri shaved her head. She would later shave her head on two additional occasions.

The daily punishments had begun almost immediately after the children were adopted. Most of the time, Immanuel and Hana had no idea why they were being punished. It could have been for standing in the wrong place or getting an answer wrong on their schoolwork. They were never quite sure.

A few months after arriving in the United States, traumatized by the change of environment and daily punishments, Immanuel began wetting the bed. Carri and Larry were convinced he was doing it on purpose just to anger them. The boy was taken outside and was given a shower with the cold hose, then sent to sleep in the dark shower room.

To add to his trauma, Carri often teased him by running the plastic tubing she called her "switch" up and down his face. On one occasion, Larry hit Immanuel on the top of the head with his fist and caused blood to run down his face. That night, he was made to sleep outside and the other children were told not to sign with him.

The punishments themselves were often straight from the *To Train Up A Child* book and involved beatings with a piece of plastic tubing that Carri kept in her bra. Sometimes it was one of Larry's belts folded in half, or a long, flexible piece of glue stick. Other common forms of punishment that the Williamses adhered to from the book included denying food, denying clothes, forced outdoor sleeping, and cold outdoor showers.

The Williams' biological children were punished, too, but never to the severity of Hana and Immanuel. The adopted children were fed different meals than the biological children. While the other children had sandwiches, Hana and Immanuel would have the same sandwich, but with a glass of water poured over it. Sometimes they would get cold leftovers with unheated frozen vegetables. Almost always, the two children were forced to eat outside while the other children ate inside, regardless of the cold, rain, or snow.

Because of Hana's menstruation, Larry and Carri took the initial steps to change her official age. Carri told her knitting group that if they could get her age bumped up a few years, they could kick her out of the house sooner when she turned eighteen. When another member of the knitting group asked how the girl would survive in the outside world, Carri snipped, "It wouldn't be my problem."

In the three years that Hana lived with the Williamses, she went from sleeping alone in the barn behind the house, to being locked inside a bathroom with no light, to eventually being kept in a four-foot by two-foot closet for up to twenty-four hours at a time. Larry's recorded bible sermons and religious music played outside of the closet the entire time, depriving her of sleep.

———

In the afternoon of Wednesday, May 11, 2011, Carri sent Hana into the backyard as one of her daily punishments. It was a rainy spring day and the temperature was in the mid-forties. When Hana, only wearing shorts and a t-shirt, complained that she was cold, Carri commanded that she do jumping jacks in the yard to stay warm. After a few hours alone outside, the children noticed Hana's lower lip quivering. She seemed unable to control her own movements, had fallen a few times, and eventually had trouble standing up at all.

Carrie went out the back door of the home and grabbed Hana by the arm and led her to the outhouse behind the barn. She continued to fall repeatedly, which infuriated Carri. She believed Hana was only trying to create attention. Unable to get her to stand, Carri left her lying alone in the yard.

Hours later, Hana's clothes were soaked. Carri set dry clothes on the back porch and yelled at her to come back inside the house. When Hana didn't return, Carri called on her two eldest sons. She gave the boys a length of plastic tubing and told them to hit her on her bottom for not following orders. Strangely, as the boys whipped her, she started to remove her own clothing and Carri called the boys back inside. By 5:00 P.M. Hana began throwing herself down on the pavement, gravel driveway, and grass. Her knees and hands began to bloody as Carri watched from inside the warm house. When she couldn't watch anymore, Carri turned away from the window and ignored Hana for the rest of the evening.

Near midnight, the seven biological Williams children giggled as they continued to stare out the window at Hana, who had removed all of her clothing and was still uncontrollably throwing her body around in a fit. She was wallowing in the mud and pounding her own head into the ground. They watched in amusement as Hana was experiencing what's known as "paradoxical undressing." In the final stages of hypothermia, the nerves can become damaged causing irrational behavior. This final stage of hypothermia tricks the mind into thinking it's extremely hot, causing the person to remove their clothes and attempt to burrow themselves into the ground.

When Hana finally stopped moving, one of the daughters called their mother to come check on Hana. She was face-down in the yard with a mouth full of mud. Carri, upset with Hana's nudity, grabbed a bedsheet and wrapped it around Hana. She then instructed her boys to drag her into the house.

First Carri called Larry, who was driving home from work. When she hung up, she finally dialed 911.

> "I think my daughter just killed herself.… She's really rebellious, and she's been outside, refusing to come in. And she's been throwing herself all around. And then she collapsed."

> "Is she breathing?"

> "I don't think so, no."

> "How old is your daughter?"

> "I don't know. We adopted her almost three years ago."

> "You don't know how old she is?"

> "She's somewhere between the ages of fourteen and sixteen. She was throwing herself all over the gravel, the yard, the patio. We went to bring her in. My sons tried to carry her in, and she took her clothes off. She's very passive-aggressive. I don't know how to describe it."

During the call, Carri sounded more annoyed than saddened or shocked. The 911 operator coached Carri through CPR, but it was no use. Hana was gone. When emergency crews arrived, Hana had a large lump on her forehead and she was covered in blood. Her hips, knees, elbows, and face had fresh red bloody markings from repeated whippings. She also had a stomach infection.

The postmortem examination of Hana's body revealed she was abnormally thin for just thirteen years old. At only five feet tall, she was emaciated and had gone back down to 76 pounds. She was lighter than 97% of girls her age and thinner than she was when she originally came from Ethiopia three years earlier. The official cause of death was hypothermia compounded by malnutrition and gastritis (stomach infection). It was determined that her body had been too thin to retain enough heat on the day she died.

When Child Protective Services knocked on the door of the Williams home the following day, Larry refused to let them in. Two weeks after Hana's death, the entire family were interviewed by detectives and Child Protective Services. All the children gave the same story, obviously coached by their parents: Hana was rebellious and "possessed by demons."

When Immanuel was interviewed, he told detectives, "People like Hana got spankings for lying and go into the fires of Hell." When Larry heard Immanuel give that answer, he immediately stopped the interview and took the children home.

Two months had gone by with no charges brought against the Williamses when Child Protective Services received an anonymous tip. Someone claimed that Carri didn't like her adopted children and Immanuel was being treated much like Hana. With that news, CPS worked with detectives and opened a formal investigation. All eight of the Williams children were taken into foster care. During a search of the house, police found a copy of the book *To Train Up a Child*.

Even after months in foster care, Immanuel was afraid of his foster parents and nervously apologized for every little mistake he made, even asking his foster mother why she wasn't beating him. He told his therapists of repeated nightmares and constantly worried that he would be the next to die. Immanuel was diagnosed with post-traumatic stress disorder.

That September, more than four months after Hana's death, Carri and Larry Williams were arrested on charges of homicide by abuse and first-degree manslaughter for the death of Hana, as well as first-degree assault of a child for the abuse of Immanuel.

Carri and Larry each faced a potential life sentence. Both posted bail of $150,000 each, but were given strict orders to not contact each other or any of their children — either directly or through third parties or other means. However, when Larry continued to send highlighted bible verses to the children, the prosecution believed them to be coded messages encouraging them to come to his defense. Larry Williams was arrested again and placed in a state jail where he remained for almost two years awaiting trial.

———

This wasn't the first time that the book by Michael and Debi Pearl, *To Train Up a Child,* had been linked to a child's death. Two other sets of fundamental Christian parents that employed tactics from the book had recently killed their adopted children:

Sean Paddock and Lydia Schatz. The three deaths happened in different parts of the United States, but all were adopted, home-schooled, and beaten with a length of 1/4 inch plastic tubing, as recommended by Michael Pearl.

Seven-year-old Lydia Schatz's parents, Kevin and Elizabeth, held her down and beat her for nine hours with a piece of the tubing for pronouncing the word "pulled" incorrectly. Four-year-old Sean Paddock's mother Lynn Paddock smothered him in a blanket wrapped too tightly around him because she wanted to stop him from getting out of bed in the middle of the night. Like Hana, the abuse that eventually killed these children was just the tip of the iceberg.

––––––––

At trial, Carri and Larry turned on each other. The couple sat at opposite tables in the courtroom, rarely looking each other in the eye. Larry testified that the discipline was all at the hands of Carri, while Carri testified that her discipline was at the instruction of her husband. Carri also admitted that she told her children not to talk to detectives about any of the abuse. The children, however, testified that lying was considered one of the most serious offenses in their household.

One of the Williams children, Joshua, confirmed that Hana had not been homeschooled or eaten meals with the other children for at least a year before her death. The child told the court that she would sometimes go two days without anyone speaking to her and none of the biological children liked her, "but it didn't matter because she was always in the closet."

Immanuel testified using sign language with the help of three interpreters. The courtroom was silent as he was asked what he thought happened to Hana. "I don't know" he signed. "She disappeared. I think maybe she's dead." He also testified that he was often beaten with a stick or plastic tubing until blood ran down his face, telling the court, "I would suffer with the pain until it eventually went away."

The biological children admitted that they were coached to tell authorities that Hana slept in the bedroom with them, when in fact she slept in a tiny locked closet. The jury was shown the closet that she slept in and were shown photos of the scars on Hana's body from repeated beatings.

Larry testified that he trusted his wife's discipline choices with the adopted children because she had done such a good job raising the other children. Carri rebutted that her husband was an equal participant in the discipline and even came up with some methods on his own, like hosing off Immanuel and locking him in the shower room after his bedwetting. She also testified that Larry was the one that installed the lock on the closet door.

During the trial, the defense attempted to argue that Hana was actually sixteen-years old rather than thirteen. If she had been sixteen at the time of her death, the homicide-by-abuse charge could not be applied as it only applies to children younger than sixteen.

Since there was no documentation of her birth from Ethiopia that proved her age either way, the trial was postponed to have Hana's body exhumed for examination. Tests on her teeth and bones, however, were inconclusive and experts couldn't confirm that she was sixteen.

The defense agreed that Larry and Carri may have been bad parents and their choices were bad, but they weren't killers and had no idea that their form of discipline would lead to the child's death.

After seven weeks of testimony, the jury didn't agree with the defense and both Larry and Carri Williams were convicted of first-degree manslaughter and first-degree assault. Carri was also found guilty of homicide by abuse and was sentenced to thirty-seven years in prison. Larry Williams was sentenced to nearly twenty-eight years and given credit for the almost two years he had been in jail awaiting trial.

———

This chapter is a free bonus chapter from True Crime Case Histories: Volume 5

Online Appendix

Visit my website for additional photos and videos pertaining to the cases in this book:

http://TrueCrimeCaseHistories.com/vol6/

More books by Jason Neal

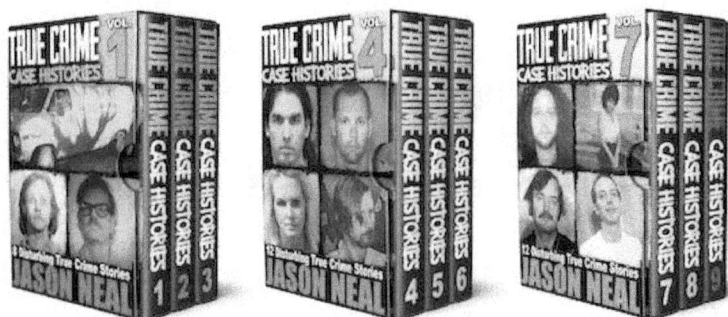

Looking for more?? I am constantly adding new volumes of True Crime Case Histories. The series **can be read in any order,** and all books are also available in paperback, hardcover, and audiobook.

Check out the complete series on Amazon

https://amazon.com/author/jason-neal

or

JasonNealBooks.com

**FREE Bonus Book
For My Readers**

**Click to get
your free copy!**

As my way of saying "Thank you" for downloading, I'm giving away a FREE true crime book I think you'll enjoy.

https://TrueCrimeCaseHistories.com

Just click the link above to let me know where to send your free book!

Choose Your Free True Crime Audiobook

Add Audible Narration and Keep the Story Going! Plus Get a FREE True Crime Audiobook!

Switch between listening to an audiobook and reading on your Kindle. **Plus choose your first audiobook for FREE!**

https://geni.us/AudibleTrueCrime

THANK YOU!

Thank you for reading this Volume of True Crime Case Histories. I truly hope you enjoyed it. If you did, I would be sincerely grateful if you would take a few minutes to write a review for me on Amazon using the link below.

https://geni.us/TrueCrime6

I'd also like to encourage you to sign-up for my email list for updates, discounts and freebies on future books! I promise I'll make it worth your while with future freebies.

http://truecrimecasehistories.com

And please take a moment and follow me on Amazon.

One last thing. As I mentioned previously, many of the stories in this series were suggested to me by readers like you. I like to feature stories that many true crime fans haven't heard of, so if there's a story that you remember from the past that you haven't seen covered by other true crime sources, please send me any details you can remember and I will do my best to research it. Or if you'd like to contact me for any other reason free to email me at:

jasonnealbooks@gmail.com

https://linktr.ee/JasonNeal

Thanks so much,

Jason Neal

ABOUT THE AUTHOR

Jason Neal is a Best-Selling American True Crime Author living in Hawaii with his Turkish-British wife. Jason started his writing career in the late eighties as a music industry publisher and wrote his first true crime collection in 2019.

As a boy growing up in the eighties just south of Seattle, Jason became interested in true crime stories after hearing the news of the Green River Killer so close to his home. Over the subsequent years he would read everything he could get his hands on about true crime and serial killers.

As he approached 50, Jason began to assemble stories of the crimes that have fascinated him most throughout his life. He's especially obsessed by cases solved by sheer luck, amazing police work, and groundbreaking technology like early DNA cases and more recently reverse genealogy.